Do IT IN PARIS

Do IT IN PARIS

An Insider's Guide to 450 Places to Visit,
Sites to See, and Things to Do

RIZZOLI
UNIVERSE

MAP *of* PARIS

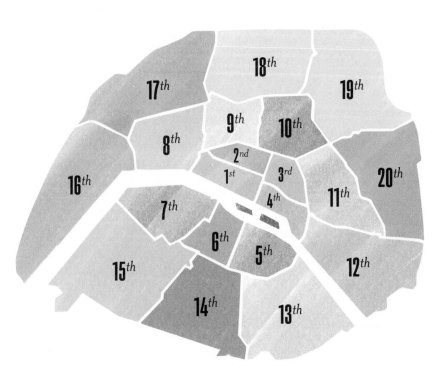

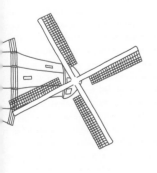

Make a date with your other half to discover a new romantic restaurant—for no reason at all. Visit that museum for the first time, just because you're passing by. Raise a glass with your BFF at a trendy cocktail bar and toast to beautiful days ahead. Snag a designer piece for a great price at a vintage boutique. Meet up with a group of friends for a picnic in a secret garden. Go for a stroll alone, staring at the sky. Take your time. Start your day gently with breakfast at a coffee shop, or grab a latte to go and sip it on your way to work. Treat yourself.

At *Do It in Paris*, we value unexpected, good ideas. Those ideas that pop into our heads and that we choose to listen to because they enhance our days, our lives. Paris never gets old—it's a city full of surprises! New, creative spots are opening all the time, as residents make their crazy dreams a reality. They're piquing our curiosity while transforming the French capital into a promised land for the small pleasures that elevate everyday life.

In this city guide, organized by neighborhoods, we'll share with you what has made our magazine so mighty. There are places that are off the beaten path, old favorites (always tested and approved by our journalists), and spots with a strong potential to become great, where we'd like to return. Treasured restaurants, stylish concept stores, pockets of nature in the heart of the city, incredible art galleries, and so much more. We suggest you make these recommendations fully your own. We want you to mark up this book, dog-ear its pages, add some memories, jot down some notes, so that it becomes a precious companion that's always by your side during your travels. It's kind of like our gift to you to thank you for supporting us all these years!

Happy strolling to all,

Clémence Renoux
Editor in Chief of Do It in Paris

CONTENTS

Auteuil
& Trocadéro

It's quite simply the chicest neighborhood
in Paris, where the main goal of walking
around is to admire the opulent buildings
and private mansions—architectural jewels
dating from the Second Empire to
the 1970s. From Place du Trocadéro
to the Bois de Boulogne, passing
through the village of Auteil, the 16th
arrondissement boasts the most beautiful
gardens and the most fascinating museums.
While they may be under the radar,
they are not to be missed.

16th Arrondissement

Clémence Renoux

OUR FAVORITE EATERIES

PARIS 16

This is a well-loved bistro—a true institution. The Dumants (of Aux Crus de Bourgogne, Les Marches) have re-created **their signature, classic roadside dining ambiance,** making liberal use of checkered tablecloths, old mirrors, wood chairs, and booths. They even have a cute, little terrace that's dreamy at sunset. The verdict: it all still works perfectly. Lovers of the hearty fare the French call *cuisine canaille* will rejoice over the vol-au-vent, tournedos of beef with bearnaise sauce, and pâté en croûte, all paired with fries that are beautifully delicate, crispy, and tender.

18 rue des Belles Feuilles, Paris 16ᵗʰ.
Bouchée à la reine €35.

FLANDRIN

Any chicer and you'll drop dead! This sophisticated, white tablecloth brasserie for the beautiful people celebrates the tradition of gorgeous Parisian restaurants. Its **seafood counter and sunny terrace** draw droves of discerning foodies and elegant tourists. Our favorite option at lunch? Roast chicken with French fries to be shared before tucking into your plus one's crème brûlée. For those into name-dropping, Flandrin's quality lies in its sourcing of ingredients, which include ice cream from Philippe Faur, coffee from Maison Verlet, and cheese from the king of fromage, Laurent Dubois.

4 place Tattegrain, Paris 16ᵗʰ.
Roast chicken for two €69.

SUBSTANCE

Top Chef junkies dutifully follow Jura-native Matthias Marc (formerly of Racines des Prés, Le Meurice, Lasserre), whose restaurant Substance is breathing new life into the Trocadéro with a young, smart team turning out playful, seasonally inspired

Flandrin / © Quentin Larcher

dishes using truly excellent ingredients, and, of course, a good dose of *vin jaune*. Here, the straightforward cuisine might include, for example, a fantastic dish of scallops with horseradish sauce, cockles, beets, and marigolds. Successful dishes are not lacking, nor is recognition—it was quick to receive its first Michelin star!
18 rue de Chaillot, Paris 16ᵗʰ.
Prix fixe lunch €62.

LE PETIT RÉTRO

An iconic spot in the 16th nestled on a discreet street, this bistro opened in 1904 is full of charm, with its lovely glazed earthenware, turquoise booths, and enormous bar. **It's a nice place to sink your teeth into delicious, retro-style** pâté en croûte, oeuf mayonnaise, sweetbreads, and hand-chopped tartare, along with a perfectly old-fashioned, delicate apple tart. Note that the authentic, classic menu was developed by the chef of Michelin-starred restaurant Chiberta, Irwin Durand, Guy Savoy's protégé.
5 rue Mesnil, Paris 16ᵗʰ.
Beef tartare €25.

MAISON REVKA

This upscale restaurant in the 16th, which draws throngs of socialites on the hunt for a good dinner, has played its part in our obsession over beautiful terraces. Its superb summer garden, where you can sit down for **a lengthy lunch under the shade of umbrellas,** resembles a painting, between the lush vegetation and the floral details on the seat cushions. With fresh fish, slender vegetables, and smooth desserts, the dishes live up to the beauty of the location. From linguine with bottarga to the signature coulibiac, everything is available with optional caviar, in the spirit of obliging service. The best option yet? Flirting at the low-lit bar as you sip a well-shaken cocktail.
59 avenue Raymond Poincaré, Paris 16ᵗʰ.
Salmon coulibiac €42.

Le Petit Rétro / © Le Petit Rétro

Maison Revka / © Romain Ricard

THE MOST BEAUTIFUL TERRACES WITH A VIEW OF THE EIFFEL TOWER

FOREST

At Julien Sebbag's restaurant, creative small plates circulate from hand to hand. The fan-favorite chef of Parisians has set up his terrace smack dab in the middle of the Musée d'Art Moderne's esplanade, which features an unobstructed view of the Eiffel Tower. One tip (actually two): reserve as early as possible and request table 100, which is best situated for admiring the view while listening to an extremely chill playlist. A veritable ode to vegetables, the dishes speak to the times, using meat and fish in their purest forms, enhanced solely by an excellent smoky sauce, along with still-crisp vegetables and other seasonal, locavore delights.

11 avenue du Président Wilson, Paris 16ᵗʰ.
Plates from €9 to €32.

LES PETITES MAINS

At the foot of the Palais Galliera, on a tree-lined square facing the Eiffel Tower, it's hard (impossible?) to find a more magnificent location than Les Petites Mains, **the pop-up terrace of the most fashionable museum in Paris.** Every summer, chefs in residence (Justine Piluso, Geoffrey Lengagne) take possession of this one-of-a-kind spot to offer Parisians an early taste of vacation. Our favorite spot? Under the columns, at the top of the stairs, overlooking the garden, with an insanely good view of the Iron Lady.

10 avenue Pierre 1ᵉʳ de Serbie, Paris 16ᵗʰ.
Lemonade €8.

SHANGRI-LA PARIS

Everyone should try the luxury hotel's La Bauhinia restaurant once in their life (at least!). It's a veritable invitation to embark on a voyage where chef Quentin Testard sets to work elevating fish with an incredibly light menu. As soon as the weather gets nice, **we book dinner in the magnificent garden,** one of the most beautiful and hidden in Paris with a view of the Eiffel Tower. Our tip? Grab an early reservation, around 7:30 p.m., so you'll have plenty of time to savor the seafood-centric menu beneath the sweet warmth of the sun: yellowtail sashimi with citrus, crispy rice and prawns, lobster ravioli, and, of course, the divine desserts by pastry chef Maxence Barbot.

10 avenue d'Iéna, Paris 16ᵗʰ.
Yellowtail sashimi with citrus €28.

Les Petites Mains / © Pierre Lucet Penato

THE BEST COCKTAILS IN WEST PARIS

SAINT JAMES PARIS

It's hard to get more romantic than Saint James! Few people know about this hotel, among the most secret in Paris, which is home to **a bar-library reminiscent of *Beauty and the Beast*.** For an elegant drink that is sure to impress your other half, you can bet on the kumquat-flavored Bellini-style cocktail (Aperol, dark rum, verjus, kumquat, blonde ale) or the Pere & Nocciole, a very smooth and tasty Manhattan (rye, poached pear, hazelnut orgeat syrup). And to go with it all: an order of pâté en croûte and a cheese plate.

5 place du Chancelier Adenauer, Paris 16ᵗʰ. Cocktails €26.

CRAVAN

People can't stop talking about the biggest cocktail bar in Paris, located in Saint-Germain-des-Prés, opened by the same team as this pocket-size bar. **But this one is still our favorite!** In this gem of a space, which has been classified as a historical monument, complete with terrace, zinc bar, and glazed earthenware,

Franck Audoux, mixologist and expert in interwar-period cocktails, disseminates his knowledge between preparations of a perfect Bloody Mary and a French 75 (giant hyssop gin, absinthe, champagne). The chicest of all? Nibbling on an uppity little snack: bottarga focaccia, leeks with mousseline sauce.

17 rue Jean de la Fontaine, Paris 16ᵗʰ. French 75 €18.

DAROCO 16

The most fashionable pizzeria in Paris has finally opened **the festive, trendy Italian restaurant** the 16th deserved. Located opposite Radio France, this restaurant—open every day for lunch and dinner—features a beautiful decor, with mirrors on the ceiling, a Klein blue mural, and a super terrace. There's also a marble cocktail bar where they'll concoct you a Campari Spritz like in Rome, or an elegant Blush (vodka, peach, strawberry, lemon) to wash down with those Bolognese arancini or the now-legendary Parmesan and rosemary focaccia. *Salute!*

3 place Clément Ader, Paris 16ᵗʰ. Cocktails €14.

Daroco 16 / © Benoît Linero

MUSEUMS WE ADORE

In addition to the Palais de Tokyo, the Fondation Louis Vuitton, and the Palais Galliera (which we clearly love), these more discreet shrines to culture delight us every time.

MAISON BALZAC

Situated in a sublime garden with a view of the Eiffel Tower, this pretty, green-shuttered residence is **the best-kept secret of the 16th.** Between 1840 and 1847, the author of *The Human Comedy* unpacked his bags here under the pseudonym "Mr. Breugnol" to get away from his creditors! In addition to exhibitions, year-round workshops, and a library that is free to the public, on the garden side you'll find the charming tearoom, Rose Bakery, which offers British-style treats, including scones and habit-forming sandwiches.
47 rue Raynouard, Paris 16th. Free entry.

MUSÉE YVES SAINT LAURENT

Welcome to the behind-the-scenes look at an iconic couture house. Prepare to get immersed in the private mansion that housed Yves Saint Laurent's headquarters until 2002! Sketches, iconic looks, vintage jewelry, personal items, archival videos, and pictures are some of the pieces that have been skillfully staged to better understand the creative process of the man who shook up the fashion world. The design studio, the great couturier's personal office, has been eerily restored so it looks as if he just left the room a moment ago.
5 avenue Marceau, Paris 16th. Full-price admission €10.

MUSÉE GUIMET

It's immense! The Musée National des Arts Asiatiques houses the most important collection in Europe, including **masterpieces from China, Korea, India, Pakistan, the Himalayas, and Japan.** The highlight of the show is the Japanese garden in the Buddhist Pavilion, a museum annex that holds tea ceremonies in a charming Chashitsu pavilion accessed from a small bamboo and stone path. It's a true Zen paradise reminiscent of a Miyazaki set.
6 place d'Iéna, Paris 16th.
Full-price admission €11.50.

MUSÉE MARMOTTAN

Lovers of impressionism, welcome to heaven. This superb museum is home to **the biggest collection of Claude Monet paintings in the world** (come here to admire *Impression, Sunrise*), in addition to mesmerizing canvases by Morisot, Renoir, Gauguin, and Caillebotte. You'll never leave empty-handed, given the amount of time you can spend in the boutique-bookstore stocking up on gifts: floral notebooks, trays, pouches, posters, and, of course, fascinating art books.
2 rue Louis Boilly, Paris 16th.
Full-price admission €14.

Musée Marmottan / © Christian Baraja SLB

Jardin des serres d'Auteuil / © Emanuela Cino

JARDIN DU PRÉ CATELAN AND JARDIN SHAKESPEARE

In the heart of the Bois de Boulogne, we love to stroll in the shade of the magnificent trees, picnic on the soft grass, and, come summer, watch a show at the outdoor theater. Actors perform amid nature in a space inspired by Shakespeare's plays, and musicians give concerts—**a simply magical evening.**

Jardin du pré Catelan, Paris 16th. Free entry.

JARDIN DU RANELAGH

It's *the* perfect spot in the 16th to lay out your towel and **put your head in a book, while perfecting your tan.** With a total surface area of fifteen acres, this la Muette green space attracts as many families (hello puppet shows!) as groups of friends who come to practice their warrior stance or engage in some open-air gossip.

1 avenue Prudhon, Paris 16th. Free entry.

JARDIN DES SERRES D'AUTEUIL

Thanks to Louis XV, who was obsessed with botany, this exotic garden has been here since 1761. Now including more than one thousand species as rare as they are spectacular, these incredible greenhouses invite you on a voyage through the continents, with giant palms, banana trees, colorful parakeets darting around in the aviaries, and a thousand other curiosities calling to mind a paradise on earth.

3 avenue de la Porte d'Auteuil, Paris 16th. Free entry.

PARC DE BAGATELLE

This botanical garden promises **a highly romantic jaunt,** given the lush vegetation, rose garden, caves, little bridges, pagoda, boulders, and waterfalls. Established following a wager between Marie-Antoinette and the Count of Artois, it took shape in just sixty-four days, done in an Anglo-Chinese style that was very fashionable at the time, in juxtaposition with Le Nôtre's orderly, symmetrical lines.

Route de Sèvres in Neuilly, Paris 16th. Full-price admission €2.50.

A DAY AT THE RACETRACK

The excitement is at its peak! Have you already dared to step through the doors of the ParisLongchamp racetrack? Betting a few bucks (or several!) on horses while having an aperitif trackside is a Parisian's favorite fancy pastime. Once there, you can get advice from pro bettors or bet on a purebred with the funniest name, all while keeping watch on the events, which change throughout the year. There are the Qatar Prix de l'Arc de Triomphe in the fall, wild nights with DJ sets every Thursday in the spring, as well as family Sundays with a ton of kid-friendly activities.

2 route des Tribunes, Paris 16th. Admission starting at €3.

Hippodrome Paris-Longchamp. © Florian Léger

MY FAVORITES

Do IT IN PARIS

MY FAVORITES

BASTILLE & ALIGRE

Around the bustling Aligre market, in the heart of the 12th arrondissement, and extending all the way to the family-friendly neighborhood surrounding the Bois de Vincennes, here are our treasured spots for dining, bargain hunting, or having a drink with a view!

Delphine Le Feuvre

OUR FAVORITE EATERIES

VIRTUS

After having taken a gander at their menu, which really smacks of the South, we were not surprised to discover that the new duo at the helm of Virtus got their start at Arnaud Donckele in Saint-Tropez. Frédéric Lorimier, who's behind the stove, and his wife, Camille Gouyer, who's at the front of the house, have successfully maintained the Michelin star that was awarded to the previous owners. At lunch, **the two menus give pride of place to Mediterranean flavors,** such as thyme-roasted saddle of lamb, slow-roasted fondant potatoes with onion and parsley, dark-roasted scallions, and grilled artichoke topped with jus and Kalamata olives.

29 rue de Cotte, Paris 12th. Prix fixe lunch €50 or €70.

BOULANGERIE COZETTE

In a corner of the 12th that's not exactly spectacular, **this neighborhood bakery offers incredible sourdough breads and high-caliber breakfast pastries.** Yet we make the trek above all for its cream puffs (vanilla, chocolate, praline), lovingly prepared by the pastry chef Paola. Hand over €2 for one of these generously filled puffs, which you can bite into on the spot or take over to the Coulée Verte, which is right in the neighborhood.

19 rue Montgallet, Paris 12th. Cream puff €2.

LE GRAND BLEU

Head toward the Arsenal boat basin, and more precisely **the little barge bridge close to the Opéra Bastille.** Go down the stairs toward the quay and you'll run into Le Grand Bleu: a high rooftop space with a clear view of the Colonne de Juillet, and a supersize terrace below where you can party—there's a place for everyone, along with a menu of Italian specialties for experiencing la dolce vita along the Seine. To digest, take a stroll alongside the boats and choose your favorite!

67 boulevard de la Bastille, Paris 12th.
Daily prix fixe menu with entrée, dessert, and coffee €19.

HUTHOPI

This is **the must-go gourmet bistro, just a stone's throw from the Bastille**: at the start of the long rue de Charenton, HuThoPi is the dream project of three childhood friends—Hugo Lafont (HU), Thomas Cuny (THO), and Pierre Le Lard (PI). The young trio sends out a magnificent prix fixe menu of appetizer, entrée, and dessert, cooked with locally sourced products and a waste-nothing philosophy, topped off with incredible service. What more could you ask for?

53 rue de Charenton, Paris 12th. Prix fixe lunch €36.

Huthopi / © Nicolas Guerbe

MAGIC CARPET CAFÉ

When we need a coffee break after making our rounds at the Aligre market, **we stop into this cozy café,** little brother to neighboring gastropub Le Singe à Paris. Incidentally, the founding owners hunted for furniture and dishes from the market's stalls, also purchasing the lovely, bold illustrations now displayed on the café's walls. Along with your cappuccino or matcha latte, order a generously sized tahini-chocolate cookie, or a piece of lemon cake topped with ultrafluffy whipped cream. Good to know: the café also serves snappy sandwiches at lunch.

5 bis rue de Prague, Paris 12th. Cookie + drip coffee combo €6 between 8 a.m. and 10 a.m.

JO AND NANA CAKES

Note to vegans who love pastries: in this tearoom with a vintage feel, beautifully decorated with flowers, you can taste the creations of chef Johanna, guaranteed to be free of animal or dairy products, along with some gluten-free options. Layer cakes, entremets, sugar-topped brioches, carrot cakes, and fun cupcakes are served on vintage porcelain. The cherry on top? A delicious brunch served daily!

14 rue Abel, Paris 12th. Brunch €29.

LE CHALET DES ÎLES DAUMESNIL

When you exit the metro, you need only take a few steps into the Bois des Vincennes to forget the frenzy of the city. The relaxed feel continues all the way to Le Chalet des Îles Daumnesnil, which was recently taken over by the Le Perchoir group. While the colorful boats cruise along Lac Daumesnil, you can grab a spot in this old nineteenth-century Swiss lodge, which has been enthusiastically transformed into a **cool country house** where you can taste the cooking of the chefs in residence. Outside, the "island cabana" features seafood products that pair marvelously with the cocktails on the menu.

Route des îles, île de Reuilly, bois de Vincennes, Paris 12th. Prix fixe lunch €55, prix fixe dinner €80.

Le Chalet des Îles Daumesnil - © Pauline Gouablin

3 ICE CREAM SHOPS
THAT MAKE US
MELT WITH JOY

LA TROPICALE
THE MOST CREATIVE

Originally located in the 13th, this long-standing family-run shop is just a stone's throw from the Viaduc des Arts: Thai-Thanh Dan's recipes are both **an invitation to travel,** as with her cà phê sữa dá (Vietnamese iced coffee), and an ode to bold pairings, as in Corsican glace à l'immortelle. We also go for its flavorful brunches and frozen mochis. In season, be sure to come early, because certain flavors usually sell out!

7 rue de Prague, Paris 12th*. 1 scoop: €3.50, 2 scoops: €5.50, 3 scoops: €7.50.*

LA GLACE ALAIN DUCASSE
THE CHICEST

Michelin-starred restaurants, bistros, a chocolate factory, a coffee factory, and now also an ice cream shop as of summer 2021: **nothing seems to be able to stop the "boss" Alain Ducasse.** Churned to order, the ice creams, sorbets, and other granitas are crafted from scratch, as pastry would be. Our favorite flavors include the interesting fresh herb sorbet, the comforting yogurt ice cream, and even the unexpected olive oil flavor.

38 rue de la Roquette, Paris 11th*. Small cup with two flavors €6.50.*

RAIMO
THE OLDEST

Since it opened in 1947 in postwar Paris, Raimo ice cream shop has been *the* **meeting place for ice cream and frozen dessert lovers** in eastern Paris. Whether you choose a cone to go or sit down to eat a cup inside the tearoom, it's impossible not to find happiness, what with the 150 flavors on the menu.

59-63 boulevard de Reuilly, Paris 12th*. 1 scoop: €4, 2 scoops: €6, 3 scoops: €8.*

WINDOW-SHOPPING

LA GALCANTE

What news made the cover of the paper the day you were born? The response to this question is certainly found in one of the tens of thousands of papers that Jacques Kuzma has collected. In this **"Gallery-Secondhand Store" specializing in birthday newspapers,** you can find press titles dated from 1920 to 2015. It's the perfect place to shop for a piece of history, whether for yourself or as a gift!

38 rue de Charenton, Paris 12th.
Classic birthday newspaper €25.

TERRA LOVA

Along with the zero-waste house opened smack dab in the middle of the 12th, now there's another place to shop **for what you need to change to a more eco-friendly lifestyle:** Marie Blandin makes soaps and shampoo and conditioner bars weekly right on-site. Our favorite? The exfoliating scrub in chocolate and coffee, made with coffee grounds recouped from a coffee roaster on the other end of the street.

67 rue de Charenton, Paris 12th.
Scrubs from €2.50.

LA BOUTIQUE SANS ARGENT

Here's a store that's one of a kind—not just in Paris, but all of France! As its name implies, you come here **to shop without a penny in your pocket.** Particularly widespread in the United States and Germany, the concept relies entirely on a gift economy: you drop off whatever items you no longer need (provided they are in good condition and don't take up too much space), and/or select items others have donated, at no cost. It's a perfect place to find a pretty cup, something for your vanity table, or a board game.

2 rue Édouard Robert, Paris 12th.

TEMPS DE TERRE

Fernanda Justina strives to bring handcrafted goods to the heart of the city. The Brazilian shop owner notably offers her "made in the 12th" **decorative stoneware and ceramics** at her studio-boutique. Do you dream of taking a turn at the wheel? Good news: classes are offered upstairs.

2 avenue Courteline, Paris 12th.
€570 for ten pottery classes.

UNTUCKED FRIPERIE

Welcome to the kingdom of secondhand! There's never any confusion here because this practical boutique offers four set prices. You'll find classic pieces for €5 or €18, while you'll need to shell out €45 for rare, so-called "iconic" pieces and €85 for luxury and collector's items. The cutting-edge selection, stunning decor, and lovely service make Untucked the place to be.

94 boulevard Poniatowski, Paris 12th.
Individual items from €5.

CŒUR GRENADINE

Need to get a gift? Look no further than this concept store (located in the spot of a former antiques shop) where Bienaimé 1935 cosmetics shares the space with chocolate bars from Chocolat des Français and teas from Maison Bourgeon, Louise Damas jewelry, stationery galore, and an inspired selection of small rugs as colorful as they are unique—all selected by Linda and Jean-Baptiste, who own a second store in Chartres.

76 avenue du général Michel Bizot, Paris 12th.

3 EXPERIENCES TO ENJOY ALONG THE VIADUC DES ARTS

It is impossible to venture into the 12th without strolling through a portion of the Coulée Verte, which runs from the Bastille to Vincennes, notably passing above the Viaduc des Arts. The boutiques inside provide a perfect opportunity to get your hands dirty!

CONFITURE PARISIENNE

Raspberry-violet, carrot-passion fruit-vanilla, strawberry-poppy—these are just a few of the original flavors cooked up at **the jam shop nestled under an arch of the Viaduc des Arts.** It also serves as a tearoom where you can enjoy a pastry. Under the jam maker's watchful eye, you can even make your own personalized jar of jam, from cutting the fruit to sealing the jar.

17 avenue Daumesnil, Paris 12th.
Gift boxes from €10.90.
Workshop €50.

LES ATELIERS CHUTES LIBRES

If you love to work with your hands, take note! You can make a wooden planter, coffee table, or even a birdhouse at this well-equipped studio, where you'll find everyone from designers to architects, cabinetmakers, and other carpenters. The raw materials used—in this case wood panels—are recovered from closing exhibitions in museums or trade fairs. **Fun and "anti-waste": we approve!**

13 avenue Daumesnil, Paris 12th, workshops from €70.

DISTILLERIE DU VIADUC

While microbreweries have been all the rage in Paris in recent years, **distilleries are having their moment within the city.** Gin, mock spirits, mint liquor, and even aquavit: everything here is made from organically grown French plants. Wishing you could make your own eau de vie? Go ahead and register for a workshop with Quentin and Théo.

55 avenue Daumesnil, Paris 12th.
A 24-oz bottle of gin du viaduc €45.
Two-hour workshop €90.

Distillerie du Viaduc / © Distillerie du Viaduc

Take a
Cultural
Break

Musée des arts forains / © Pavillons de Bercy

LA CINÉMATHÈQUE FRANÇAISE

Housed inside a building designed by architect Frank Gehry, this wonderful destination for cinephiles offers thematic retrospectives (like espionage cinema), as well as **fascinating exhibitions.** Musée Méliès inside the Cinémathèque is by itself worth the detour, revealing all the magic tricks of the movies, with more than three hundred machines, costumes, posters, drawings, and models displayed over an 8,600-sq.-ft space.

51 rue de Bercy, Paris 12th. Ticket for exhibition + museum €16.

MUSÉE DES ARTS FORAINS

While it might very well be the most poorly situated museum in the capital—stuck between Bercy Village and the highway, it is definitely the most unusual! From the moment you enter, you're immersed in a dreamlike world that presents surprise after surprise. You can delve into the "Venetian fairs" with a larger-than-life Rialto Bridge, or climb aboard **a hundred-year-old merry-go-round in the middle of an old-fashioned carnival.** It's a must-see trip back in time!

53 avenue des Terroirs de France, Paris 12th. Visit by reservation only (€18.80 per adult ticket).

The People Nation / © Girette

L'HÔTEL MK2 PARADISO

Perched atop the MK2 Nation movie theater and the Hôtel Paradiso, this verdant rooftop only opens when the weather is nice, so Parisians and travelers alike can enjoy the 360-degree view surrounding it. If heading up to seventh heaven (the seventh floor) is not enough, there are also **outdoor movie screenings.** Every summer, those lucky enough to snag a drink reservation on the roof can enjoy a weekly film beneath the stars. Awesome!

135 boulevard Diderot, Paris 12ᵗʰ.
Sunday screening + drink €18.

THE PEOPLE PARIS NATION

For an aperitif with a view of all of Paris, meet up on the sixth floor of the youth hostel The People. The food menu takes us right to Italy with burrata, pizza, and spritzes galore, all prepared exclusively with local products. Our insider tip? Come during the day—the view is just as stunning and definitely clearer! La Défense, the Montparnasse Tower, the Eiffel Tower, Montmartre, and, of course, Place de la Nation—you'll get all the Parisian monuments at once.

28 bis place de la Nation, Paris 12ᵗʰ.
Reservations not accepted. Italian brunch €30.

BATIGNOLLES

Is it really just "Strollerland"? So
nicknamed for its strong appeal to families,
this arrondissement-village tucked between
the chic 16th and the more "bobo" 18th has
way more hidden gems and good deals than
you might think. Romantic squares, trendy
shopping, and gourmet eateries—
your visit has begun!

17th & 18th Arrondissements

Céline Dassonville

OUR FAVORITE EATERIES

LE FAHAM

Before this place got its Michelin star, it was a love story between Kelly Rangama, former Top Chef contestant, and Jérôme Devreese, a pastry chef who'd cooked at all the luxury hotels. Together, they came up with this light-filled jewel box of a restaurant. And the food? **It's a very personal** *cuisine d'auteur,* **with exotic accents.** Three-, four-, or five-course menus provide nothing short of a feast, between the succulent *sarcives,* marinated pork shoulder chops, tandoori squid, or the irresistible aged Cour d'Armoise chicken.
108 rue Cardinet, Paris 17th. Five-course prix fixe €102.

KRISPY KOREAN KITCHEN

Meet Parisians' latest street food obsession: **chimaek, that delicious fried chicken** paired with a nice, cold beer. To eat it as they do in Seoul, head toward Krispy Korean Kitchen, the long-awaited brick-and-mortar shop of the eponymous food truck. Tender inside with a crispy outside thanks to a special (flour-free)

coating and double frying, it arrives enveloped in sweet-and-sour sauces (spicy or mild). Everything comes with rice and/or house-made fries, and the space has a charming, greasy spoon vibe.
22 rue Biot, Paris 17th. Krispy Meal €14.

VALMA

Home cooking with fresh, seasonal products, including for kids: that's the mission statement of this busy cafeteria, which is a top pick for parents keen on eating well. We love the comforting little dishes and tasty pastries served here seven days a week, but nothing beats the gigantic weekend brunch! Nice touch: the restaurant's annex can be rented out to celebrate a little one's birthday.
34 rue Lemercier, Paris 17th. Prix fixe brunch €25.

MONTIJO

In a setting evocative of a wine shop, the restaurant at the Maison Eugénie hotel is **a buzzworthy spot to sip an aperitif.** You can share generous portions of tapas (pan con tomate, a just-cooked tortilla Española, jamon ibérico, sheep's milk cheeses, etc.), which you can enjoy with fantastic sangria topped off with apricot syrup and tonic. The best place to snag a seat? The airy veranda filled with gorgeous plants is the perfect comfy spot.
167 rue de Rome, Paris 17th.
Iberian charcuterie board €28.

Montijo / © Montijo

4 COFFEE SHOPS
WHERE YOU
FEEL GOOD

MAISON DIMANCHE

Originally a bakery with sections of organic sourdough bread sold by weight, this place has now morphed into a gourmet coffee shop. You can sip a matcha or frothy macchiato while enjoying the country-style decor (owner Guillaume Martin loves his bric-a-brac). For baked goods, the bar is high: **salted butter caramel cookies, giant palmiers, and chocolate babkas.** Not to be missed: the cinnamon or chocolate pistachio buns. Yummmmm!

1 rue Tarbé, Paris 17th and 147 bis rue Cardinet, Paris 17th. Bun €3.50.

LA MAIN NOIRE

This terrace at the foot of the Montmartre cemetery has umbrellas as vividly striped as the ones on the cabanas in Brighton Beach! With its underground test kitchen, La Main Noire promises **quality products, hyperlocal sourcing, and artisanal expertise.** The sweet and savory pancakes and sticky chai granola call for one of the creamy, colored potions—a green matcha, black charcoal, or yellow turmeric latte. One cool touch: you can purchase some of the products to use at home, including its famous roasted black sesame paste.

12 rue Cavallotti, Paris 18th. Golden latte €4.

LA PÉPINIÈRE DES BATIGNOLLES

It's impossible to miss this place, what with its facade painted with birds of paradise. Similar to other coffee shops where it's nice to chill out, La Pépinière des Batignolles offers a tropic-cool ambiance with rattan armchairs and hanging plants. The café turns out **flat whites, iced teas, and other fresh juices,** alongside pure butter madeleines, and slices of chocolate marble loaf or fromage blanc cakes. Also high on our lunch-hour list: the must-have avocado toast and vegan bowls.

15 rue des Dames, Paris 17th. Matcha latte €5.50.

DOSE

Behind the Sainte-Marie-des-Batignolles church, **coffee enthusiasts stand firm:** it's Dose and nowhere else that makes the best java, such as Peruvian spiced with notes of caramel and almonds and fruity from Ethiopia with peach and vanilla aromas. The microroaster sells elixirs you'd sell your soul for. The line at the take-out counter each morning speaks for itself! As for the food, the granolas, cookies, and pastries are all homemade in its kitchen right down the street.

82 place du docteur Félix Lobligeois, Paris 17th. Espresso to go €1.50, cake of the day €3.50.

La Main Noire / © Pepa

A Historic Hotel

L'Eldorado / © Benoît Linero

L'ELDORADO

Fans of minimalism, be on your way! The latest (big) baby from Moussié and Sophie Richard (to whom we owe the Providence hotel), L'Eldorado, a historic hotel in Batignolles, has undergone the ultimate facelift and become the most popular spot of the summer in the process. People are rushing here from the opposite end of Paris to discover its new restaurant, which boasts a palm-shaded terrace (club sandwich, eggs mimosa, vegetable tempura, etc.), while the unique rooms offer a low-lit vision of Parisian romance. Vintage rattan furniture, magnificent velvet tapestries on the walls, terraces, and windows with a view of the treetops so you can awake to birdsong. Or engage in the art of melding country spirit with Parisian extravagance.

18 rue des Dames, Paris 17ᵗʰ. Rooms from €350. Spaghetti with bottarga €26.

THE CRÈME DE LA CRÈME

BOULANGERIE BAPTISTE

THE BEST BAKERY IN THE NEIGHBORHOOD

Batignolles, a brand-new land for food artisans? After pastry celebrities Jeffrey Cagnes and Yann Couvreur, enter *Meilleur Ouvrier de France* titleholder Joël Defives, the master baker and former executive chef at the Thierry Marx bakeries. Behind an art deco facade, his bakery, coined Baptiste in homage to his adopted son, **is championing the best French artisanal baking.** Every item is prepared with long-fermented ancient grains. Don't leave until you've tried the chef's point of pride: his signature Baptiste bread. It's a sober, aromatic bread, made to be buttered with joy.

17 rue des Moines, Paris 17ᵗʰ. Traditional baguette €1.30.

FORMATICUS

SIGNATURE CHEESES

A sixth-generation cheese producer, the Lincet family opened its wine bar in... an old butcher shop! On the menu: **the best fromages from here to the moon,** via the shortest possible supply chain. Must-tries: the Chaource, Epoisses, truffled Brillat-Savarin, as well as the Cantal, Saint-Nectaire, and Mont D'Or. Unforgettable: the Gouda, aged forty-eight months with salt crystals that crunch beneath your teeth. Add to that a lovely wine list and great staff and you have one of the most desirable and authentic places in the neighborhood.

16 rue Brochant, Paris 17ᵗʰ. Board with six cheeses €27.

WINDOW-SHOPPING

DÉSORDRE URBAIN

Depression be gone! Here they cultivate a spirit of good vibes, with bold colors and fun objects. The selection: costume jewelry, fashion accessories, stationery, and decor, all laid out bric-a-brac style. On our wish list: a pair of green Feeka resin earrings, a Bindi Atelier printed pouch, a cotton Mapoésie scarf, and a rhinestone Les Femmes à Barbe barrette. *96 rue Nollet, Paris 17ᵗʰ. &Klevering vase €40.*

LA RESSOURCERIE DES BATIGNOLLES

Head here for good deals! Beyond Porte d'Asnières, the former Free Market de Paname has set up shop in this hybrid space, which is half vintage store, half soup kitchen. From a leather couch to a vintage shirt, not to mention the selection of vinyl records, tableware, and kitschy home items, we love to rummage and uncover soulful hidden gems here. Great finds include special sale items from luxury houses like Chanel, Cacharel, and Alaïa that won't have you dipping into your savings account. *132 rue de Saussure, Paris 17ᵗʰ. Mug €1.50.*

VILLA GYPSY

Decorated like a hut, this boutique doubles as a café offering excellent healthy bites (lentil salad with smoked salmon, chicken Colombo) and a coffee shop where you can slow down and enjoy a chai latte. As far as the shopping goes, **the delightfully bobo selection has much to recommend it:** embroidered cushions, ceramic bud vases, wicker baskets, and Kodama teas—we love it all! *126 rue Legendre, Paris 17ᵗʰ. Beaded lobster & crab pouches €27.50.*

BLOU

The Marais has its Fleux store, and Batignolles has Blou. Opened in 2010, this temple to design with three stores on rue Legendre is a point of reference for lovers of beautiful, functional objects. We stroll through as if it was a museum to admire designer pieces from the likes of Vitra, Petite Friture, Hay, or even Treku. Inside tip: floor samples are discounted, sometimes to as low as 60 percent off. *97 and 99 rue Legendre, Paris 17ᵗʰ. Panthella table lamp by Louis Poulsen €270.*

COLORTHERAPIS

This creative studio hidden away on rue Davy offers **pop and vintage pieces to fend off the doldrums.** The inspo? A mixture of Bauhaus-inspired shapes paired with a color palette that conjures up Matisse. Vintage armchairs from the 1960s and 1970s found in Romania, from where founder Lavinia originally hails, have been reupholstered in swathes of fabric from the great fashion houses: Courrèges, Pierre Frey, and Kenzo. The studio also designs incredible tufted rugs, which are made in India using the finest New Zealand wool. The best part: you can order a custom-designed rug, choosing from over 1,800 color options. *35 rue Davy, Paris 17ᵗʰ. Armchairs €429.*

Color therapis / © ColorTherapis

KID-FRIENDLY KID-FRIENDLY

Le pestacle de Maëlou / © Le pestacle de Maëlou

LE PESTACLE DE MAËLOU

Neighborhood parents swear by this pastel-colored spot boasting **a high cuteness factor.** Devoted to the littlest shoppers (ages newborn to five), this boutique is a gold mine of fun and ethically sourced treasures, where you are sure to find the perfect baby gift, from So Family cotton sleepsacks to Liewood sustainable pacifiers, not to mention those indispensable Jellycat lovies. The owners, who are always up-to-the-minute on trends, bend over backward to provide the best advice.

92 rue Legendre, Paris 17ᵗʰ. Jellycat bunny stuffed toy €29.

EMILE ET IDA

And then there were three! After the first store on rue de Richelieu and the second one on rue Montmartre, the children's clothing brand founded by Delphine Papiernik continues its irresistible rise with this new light-filled jewel of a store. The racks hold **the fanciful clothes** that made the brand famous: delicate blouses with embroidered buttons, smocked little skirts, sweet colors, and floral prints. All items are produced in limited quantities and are impeccably finished.

83 rue Nollet, Paris 17ᵗʰ. Cotton bloomers €45.

LA SARDINE À LIRE

Émilie and Léa, fans of children's literature, took over this too-cute neighborhood bookstore with its floor tiles and themed window display, which changes monthly. The selection of five thousand titles gives pride of place to independent publishers: Biscotto, Les Fourmis Rouges, Hélium–Tchoupi, and Petit Ours Brun are so yesterday! **You'll find playground stars** (yoohoo Mortelle Adèle), a well-stocked manga section, along with costume jewelry, stuffed animals, and dress-up clothes.

4 rue Colette, Paris 17ᵗʰ.
Anatole Latuile, *Volume 16 €11.50.*

BISCUIT

In addition to its outpost in the 11th, Biscuit has opened a Batignolles location featuring its creative concept for young and old alike: **paint-your-own ceramics.** The method: you choose an unglazed object (mug, egg cup, vase, etc.) and then decorate it however you want using glazes, sponges, or stencils. All of the materials are available on-site. Once your item has been glazed and fired, you come pick it up a few days later.

121 rue Legendre, Paris 17ᵗʰ. Parent-child workshop €60.

SCENIC

STROLLS

LA CITÉ DES FLEURS

A breath of the country in the middle of Paree! Those in the know love this quaint private path, which is accessible during the day to those visiting the passage. With **its private mansions, balconies filled with wisteria, and lazy cats,** it's a haven of peace far from the Paris frenzy. We love to take a stroll here and stop for a coffee, or take a romantic walk on a Sunday to admire the place where the painter Alfred Sisley lived and Catherine Deneuve and Françoises Dorléac were born.

Entrance at 154 avenue de Clichy, Paris 17ᵗʰ.

LE SQUARE DES BATIGNOLLES

David vs. Goliath. Opposite the giant Martin Luther King park, **this beautiful English garden puts up a good fight!** It must be said that the nerve center of Batignolles was built to please, with its river, waterfall, and old-fashioned merry-go-round. We come to whisper sweet nothings on benches along the Allée Barbara, opposite hundred-year-old plane trees and ducks splashing around in the lake. It's also a popular spot for pétanque, with two courts that delight fans when the weather is good.

144 bis rue Cardinet, Paris 17ᵗʰ.

LE BAL

A LOVELY BOOKSHOP

Hidden along a dead-end cobblestone street, this is *the favorite meeting place for the neighborhood's artsy set.* A former brothel that became the largest off-track-betting facility in France, the spot embraced its new destiny in 2010 when Diane Dufour and Raymond Depardon opened Le Bal, a pocket-size museum dedicated to visual arts (photography, video, new media, etc.) with a societal, engagement-focused bent. The programming is cutting-edge and radical. Artistically, it runs the gamut, from the emerging international scene and forgotten figures of photography to research on forms, holding exhibitions every three months and two festivals a year. What we love: the pretty bookstore at the entrance and the tiny adjacent restaurant run by the Le Récho association, which helps refugees train for restaurant jobs. On the menu: seasonal dishes inspired by the market and far-off countries.

6 impasse de la Défense, Paris 18th.
Full-price ticket to museum €8.
À la carte menu €8 to €17.

Le BAL / © Marc Domage

BELLEVILLE
& MÉNILMONTANT

Discover the Parc des Buttes Chaumont
and its bucolic grounds; Belleville, with its
Asian restaurants and artists' studios; or
Ménilmontant, with its vintage spirit.
Take a quick lap around one of these
thriving neighborhoods—they're trendy
diamonds in the rough that are bursting
with authentic spots.

19th & 20th Arrondissements

Clara Caggini

OUR FAVORITE EATERIES

AUX FOLIE'S

With its decor featuring tiles, collages, and legendary red neon signs, this neighborhood institution draws intellectual philosopher types from the Sorbonne, poets, and artists, not to mention groups of friends passing by. The extremely nice service and relaxed atmosphere make it **a superfriendly bar, where you always meet great people,** right down to the spacious and perpetually packed terrace where the tables mingle with one another whether it's summer or winter (when the terrace is heated). That's the spirit of Belleville! In the afternoon, we love to sip its famous house-made mint tea. In the evenings, under the wam glow of the red lights, enjoy a petit jaune or pastis water made with the aniseed-flavored liqueur Pernod, ice cubes, and water.

8 rue de Belleville, Paris 20th.
Mint tea €2.50.

SOCES

Working as an oyster seller has never been so seductive! Located in the very hip neighborhood of Jourdain, this bistro-wine cellar elevates lovely shellfish in seasonal dishes that vary depending on what's available. Must-tries include swoon-worthy spicy oyster amuse-bouches, Groix mussels with a creamy marinière sauce topped with sausages, and absolutely not to be missed: the insanely good poached pear and praline napoleon.

32 rue de la Villette, Paris 19th.
Mussels marinière with sausage €14.

FLORÉAL BELLEVILLE

This old bistro decorated in bric-a-brac is both an art gallery and cultural hub. It offers **a peaceful haven for happy hour and brunches.** Indulge without moderation in small share plates such as Pouilles burrata paired with honey-roasted blood oranges or smashed sweet potatoes with bottarga and citrus. We never miss its year-round events like concerts and clothing swaps, which are announced a few days prior on social media.

43 rue des Couronnes, Paris 20th. Sunday brunch €25.

Floréal Belleville / © Floréal Belleville

LA ROSE DE TUNIS

Craving a little treat? This **Tunisian bakery-pastry shop** may not look like much from the outside, but it's a journey through a tale from *One Thousand and One Nights*. The diet-be-damned delights include baklava triangles dripping with honey, semolina pastry with dates (makroud), and almond horns galore. Savory options include a swoon-worthy Tunisian flatbread. You'll leave with semolina breads and pastries to gorge on at home that night, if you can even make it until then.

67 boulevard de Belleville, Paris 11th. Baklava €1.

FIVE TRAVEL-INDUCING RESTAURANTS

LE PRÉSIDENT

It's almost impossible to miss this enormous restaurant situated at the intersection of boulevard and rue de Belleville. The grand entrance, complete with an oversize staircase in traditional colors, is straight out of a movie set. Indeed, the extravagant ambiance is the first indication of the high-caliber cooking. On the menu: **head to Canton with seafood specialties** like the chef's special breaded shrimp, scrambled eggs with prawns, or soy sauce turbot, paired with delicious noodles.

120-124 rue du Faubourg du Temple, Paris 11ᵗʰ. Breaded shrimp €12.

LE ROULEAU DE PRINTEMPS

If you happen to be in the 20th, this **inexpensive hole-in-the-wall is a must.** It's a neighborhood eatery where everything's good and prices are easy on the wallet. You'll first need to make the climb from Belleville, but it's worth the effort. On the menu: spring rolls to wrap in lettuce and dip in tangy sauce, thin rice noodles in every form, and dumplings. Added plus: there are plenty of vegetarian options, between the stir-fried noodles, croquettes, and chive pancakes.

42 rue de Tourtille, Paris 20ᵗʰ. Shrimp dumplings €4.60.

CHEVAL D'OR

This restaurant in Haut Belleville has been generating a buzz with **its French- and Japanese-influenced share plates.** Have a seat in the pared-down setting, and enjoy refined dishes like mussels and asparagus with Szechuan chili oil, or excellent ramen. We particularly appreciate the lovely old-fashioned blue porcelain tableware. The specialty? Tsukune, delicious chicken meatballs on skewers, served with teriyaki sauce and an egg yolk.

21 rue de la Villette, Paris 19ᵗʰ. Tsukune €14.

LAO SIAM

Pad thai enthusiasts are in seventh heaven at this cult favorite in the 20th, which serves Lao and Thai cuisine. We strongly suggest you reserve in advance, so you can enjoy sweet and savory dishes like the salad of banana flower, coconut, and shrimp, or the chicken with tamarind, basil, and pineapple. Those with a sweet tooth will love the tapioca pearls with coconut milk and banana.

49 rue de Belleville, Paris 19ᵗʰ. Pad thai €12.80.

CHINA TOWN

Come here to experience peak kitsch. Nestled right in the heart of Belleville, **this wild karaoke bar is an unexpected epicenter of Parisian trendsetters** (we've seen the team from *Vogue* there). At this often-inundated spot (reserve ahead!) you can sit as a group around large tables with lazy Susans to share a dish of insanely good shaking beef or dumplings in between attempts at Britney songs.

27 rue du Buisson Saint-Louis, Paris 10ᵗʰ. Shrimp with spicy sauce €15.

Chinatown / © Emanuela Cino

LE FOOD MARKET  STREET FOOD

Yummm. This street food market is *the* **monthly meeting spot for culinary debauchery at superlow prices,** and with music too, if you like. Watch out for the schedule on social media, and set aside an evening to stroll among the stalls of Couronnes and Ménilmontant. Surrender to the most tantalizing aromas from the stands, which are different each time depending on the theme (Italian gastronomy, Chinese New Year, etc.) Behind the stoves: top chefs from Michelin-starred restaurants, cosmopolitan food trucks, and neighborhood eateries.

On boulevard de Belleville between the Couronnes and Ménilmontant metro stations. Free admission, dishes €10 –15.

3 ENTICING
Brunches

Benoît Castel / © Guillaume Czerw

MARDI

Between Buttes Chaumont and Haut Belleville lies **a true gathering place, where you can brunch, work, and linger with friends on the weekend.** The tasty menu includes a granola and yogurt parfait or soft-boiled eggs with *comté* cheese, whipped butter, and slices of buckwheat bread for breakfast. At brunch and teatime, you'll find timeless classics like cheesecake (the restaurant's most popular dessert), Stockholm-inspired vegetarian creations, along with stracciatella-honey tartines, a soup of the day, and cinnamon rolls.

29 rue de la Villette, Paris 19th.
Soft-boiled egg with sides €8.

THE DANCING GOAT

Nestled a few steps away from Place Gambetta, this spot, which draws in the Carrie Bradshaws of the 20th, is **a sweet mix of British pub, New York café, and French bistro.** Lulled throughout the day by the sounds of a jazz band, we order the eye-catching house-made pastries to stay: cookies, cakes (the orange cake is incredible, as is the coconut!), marble cake, or a chocolate brownie, all washed down with a cappuccino, an excellent iced matcha latte, or a freshly squeezed orange juice.

117 avenue Gambetta, Paris 20th.
Cookie €3.

BENOÎT CASTEL

We knew the rue de Ménilmontant location well, as it became a neighborhood institution, with its all-you-can-eat brunch featuring salads, charcuterie, cheeses, quiche, pizza, seasonal soups, and pastries galore. A little further up in the 20th, **the French bakery guru** has struck again with L'Alimentation, its grocery shop, which offers everything you need to re-create your Sunday brunch at home. Not to be missed!

150 rue de Ménilmontant, Paris 20th.
All-you-can-eat brunch €35.
L'Alimentation, 11 rue Sorbier, Paris 20th.

VILLA RIBEROLLE

SIGNATURE COOKING

Against a timeless rustic backdrop, these long-standing workers' haunts made over into charming cottages are home to the top cuisine d'auteur spots of the moment, including these three favorites.

Cache / © Maki Manoukian

CACHÉ

To find the entrance, you need only follow the seasonal bouquets laid out on the path leading to the large glass room. Opened by trendy chef Lorenza Lenzi, this spot offers **of-the-moment dishes featuring fresh fish,** which change depending on what has come in that day. We're crazy for both the checkered sea bream sashimi, a graphic composition you dip into the accompanying yuzu and miso sauce, and, of course, the delicious ahi tuna tataki. Kudos to the divine cocktails, which pair perfectly with the menu.

23 Villa Riberolle, Paris 20ᵗʰ.
Royal sea bream sashimi €35.

SANTA SILVIA

Located in an old barn, Santa Silvia plays up its **refined Italian trattoria** vibe with a short seasonal menu served in a superfriendly setting to a soundtrack of Pino d'Angio

hits (such passion). The tasty menu features classic appetizers from the boot-shaped country, like vitello tonnato, bruschetta, or a crudo showcasing the fish of the day, as well as a wide range of pastas, including ravioli all'amatriciana and pasta alla Norma, reinvented with gooey stracciatella cheese.

22 Villa Riberolle, Paris 20ᵗʰ. Pasta alla Norma €18.

AMAGAT

Fans of **Spanish wine cellars** find refuge at this lovely hideout with glass bay windows overlooking a cobblestoned court. Here you can share a selection of Iberian charcuterie and tiny sardines with peppered butter, along with a nice vermouth. We order plate after plate of the insanely good tapas, such as the famous croquetas topped with spicy sauce and aioli, or an excellent tortilla like the ones in Barcelona, all cooked up by Catalan chef Sylvain Roucayrol (formerly of Experimental).

23 Villa Riberolle, Paris 20ᵗʰ. Croquetas €4.

MY FAVORITES
DO IT IN
PARIS
MY FAVORITES

A Walk in the Park

Parc de Belleville / © Emanuela Cino

LE PARC DE BELLEVILLE

We love this park as much for its free concerts when the weather is nice as for its minimarkets every weekend at Belvédère, complete with a panoramic view of the capital. Not to be missed: Grab food for a picnic from the Asian take-out shops on rue de Belleville or snag a seat on one of the long terraces at the Moncœur or Les Bols d'Antoine bar-restaurants to take advantage of the relaxed ambiance on rue Piat.

78 rue Georges Lardennois, Paris 19th.
47 rue des Couronnes, Paris 20th.

LES BUTTES CHAUMONT

With its romantic pavilion and giant, gently sloping lawns, this is **a perfect place for a picnic.** You'll also find several rustic *guinguettes*, including Pavillon Puebla (run by the team from Perchoir), which delivers great pizzas and a memorable Moscow mule. And for a different vibe, check out another bar, Rosa Bonheur, which opened its festive space at the top of the park. It's the ideal spot to grab a beer as the sun is going down. Note: the park stays open 24-7 in summer.

Place Armand-Carrel, Paris 19th.

LA BUTTE BERGEYRE

This is **one of the neighborhood's best-kept secrets.** And rightly so, because this lovely garden is truly an extension of the Buttes Chaumont. With its panoramic view, it's *the* spot par excellence to see fireworks on Bastille Day! Given the small space, seats are rare and the crowd spills out onto the lawn on French Independence Day. Our tip: get there early!

78 rue Georges Lardennois, Paris 19ᵗʰ.

AND ALWAYS...

From the foot of Père-Lachaise, we walk to **Jardin Naturel Pierre Emmanuel** (*120 rue de la Réunion — 12 ter rue de Lesseps, Paris 20ᵗʰ*) for its rare exotic plants, or to **Villa de l'Ermitage** (*Paris 20ᵗʰ*), which cultivates a country village spirit with its shared gardens. A bit further down, on rue des Vignoles (*Paris 20ᵗʰ*), the dead-end roads filled with flowers remain well protected from the chaos of the capital.

3 MUST-SEE GALLERIES TO DISCOVER

There's more to life than the Marais! Between the need for space and a desire to be in an artsy neighborhood that has its finger on the pulse, hip galleries have moved into Belleville in recent years. These three amazing gulleries provide proof of concept.

Galerie Crèvecoeur / © Emanuela Cino

GALERIE CRÈVECŒUR

In addition to taking part in the most prestigious contemporary art fairs, this gallery has an outpost on both banks of the river, with another location in the 7th. Hidden in the courtyard of a building in the same neighborhood as the Hermitage, this light-filled space showcases **new artists to watch.**

9 rue des Cascades, Paris 20th.

GALERIE 22,48 M²

A real gem that is worth the detour! Its goal? To represent young French artists and **push research into artificial intelligence in art** while collaborating with some of today's most sought-after curators to create the exhibitions.

30 rue des Envierges, Paris 20th.

GALERIE MARCELLE ALIX

This up-and-coming gallery is managed by a pair of bold women who are challenging the art market with their creative verve. The space, designed completely lengthwise, welcomes impressive installations and colorful works in an amazing setting.

4 rue Jouye-Rouve, Paris 20th.

WE'D CROSS PARIS FOR . . .

LE PAVILLON CARRÉ DE BAUDOUIN

While the 20th has long been a favorite arrondissement of artists, it was still missing a cutting-edge exhibition site. No longer, now that we have **this villa-museum right in the heart of Paris.** This eighteenth-century pleasure palace, once a residence of the Goncourt brothers and used as a formal home, has been renovated to host a variety of exhibitions and conferences. The imposing Palladian-inspired building with grounds filled with gardens, and the villa, are free and open to the public.

121 rue de Ménilmontant, Paris 20th.
Free admission.

KO HANA

FOR HAUTE-COUTURE BOUQUETS

This boutique might just outshine celebrity florists Castor and Debeaulieu. In addition to floral art, to which only the Japanese hold the key, Ko Hana also offers **handcrafted ceramics made on-site,** which further elevate its bouquets. The studio has notably won over many Parisian designers, with arrangements featuring beautiful seasonal stems for fashion week events.

36 avenue Simon Bolivar, Paris 19th. Seasonal bouquet €40.

LA BELLEVILLOISE

DEN OF THE PARTYGOERS

The first worker's cooperative to be established in 1877, La Bellevilloise has always maintained its role as a cultural agitator. This exciting spot books **lively workshops, conferences, and concerts.** For clubgoers: electronica, swing, or Brazilian music sets appear one after the other, depending on the night. Special nod to the onstage spaces, which feature a large terrace and a lounge corner with couches where you can sit down with friends and sip your drink. And that's not all: on Sundays, enjoy jazz and brunch beneath the shade of olive trees.

19-21 rue Boyer, Paris 20th. Admission €7 to €20.

DIY COURSES TO TRY OUT STAT

Need to unwind? Here's **a hip and comforting activity** to free your inner artist. In her studio located next to Père-Lachaise, **Laurette Broll** uses her superior teaching skills to introduce neophytes how to craft ceramic objects, from modeling to glazing, at weekly classes and weekend intensives. Added bonus? The on-site boutique sells handmade plates, carafes, and mugs.

47 avenue Gambetta, Paris 20th. €170 for three weekly classes.

© Emanuela Cino

Butte-aux-Cailles & Gobelins

The village feel in Butte-aux-Cailles makes it a great place to live; passersby walk along streets scrawled with street art, bobos cruise by on bikes, kids play in the street, and bon vivants gather around for a pint at a terrace bar. It's a true taste of the country right in Paris!

13th & 14th Arrondissements

Pauline de Quatrebarbes

Dame Augustine / © Studio La Rivière

DAME AUGUSTINE

Welcome to the neighborhood gourmet spot owned by **Top Chef Lilian Douchet** (season thirteen), which recently celebrated its first birthday. The restaurant has become a true foodies' den, with its floral decor and impeccably sourced seasonal menu. You'll find soft-boiled egg with smoked trout, tender monkfish with green apple sauce, or roasted poultry with a fermented sauce. So good!

32 avenue des Gobelins, Paris 13th.
Prix fixe lunch €28 during the week.

LES CAILLOUX

Come *aperitivo* time, meet up at this incredibly warm and **homey trattoria,** which offers all the best specialties from Italy: fine antipasti, paccheri with shrimp, vitello tonnato, and linguine cacio e pepe. And if you still have room, there's a classic tiramisu.

58 rue des Cinq Diamants, Paris 13th.
Pastas €16 to €19. Tiramisu €9.

HOT SPOTS

It always feels like a party in Butte-aux-Cailles! Anyone who's anybody in Paris is there, glasses in hand, to enjoy a great night out with a group of friends. Start at **La Folie en Tête** (*33 rue de la Butte aux Cailles, Paris 13th*), which has a lively atmosphere and musical instruments blanketing the walls. Then head over to **Merle Moqueur** (*11 rue de la Butte aux Cailles, Paris 13th*), which is well known for its trendy selection of rums, ti' punch, and draft beers, at unbeatable prices. End with a drink at **Le Mêlécasse** (*12 rue de la Butte aux Cailles, Paris 13th*), the true epicenter of the neighborhood, which offers an immense terrace that runs the length of the bistro.

Le Mêlécasse / © Emanuela Cino

CULTURAL IMMERSION

Pourquoi pas ? © Emanuela Cino

POURQUOI PAS ?

This art gallery-antique store brimming with beautiful items feels like an **express journey to all four corners of the globe.** Stroll through the immense two-floor hangar and admire African or Balinese treasures you can't find anywhere else, along with many other gems inspired by non-European art. Globe-trotters will adore decorating their homes with these unique items, which all have that soulful je ne sais quoi.

31 rue Vergniaud, Paris 13th. Free admission.

LES FLOCATS

In this **studio-boutique dedicated to mosaics,** Catherine and Florence offer the friendliest classes in Paris. We must say that these two former illustrators from Walt Disney Studios are not lacking in ideas to boost their hardworking students' creativity. But if DIY is not your thing, the boutique offers loads of lovely items (mirrors, tables, etc.) that have already been customized.

43 rue Vandrezanne, Paris 13th. €50 for a three-hour course, €192 for the complete twelve-hour cycle.

LE LAVO//MATIK

Fans of urban art flock to this **avant-garde gallery-bookstore,** whose immense collection of books is a point of reference. The under-the-radar space offers new exhibitions each month, where new names in street art come to mingle among graffiti, painting, and sculpture works from the world scene.

20 boulevard du Général d'Armée Jean Simon, Paris 13th. Free admission.

STREET ARTIST CENTRAL

They're the soul of the neighborhood: Butte-aux-Cailles is home to a ton of artworks you can admire in the street for free, signed by major names in street art, from Miss.Tic to Space Invader, not to mention Kashink, Jef Aérosol, and Toc Toc.

© Emanuela Cino

A mural on rue de l'Espérance, which is also home to works by Sarce, Rémi Cierco, Lex, and Jef Aérosol
↓

The famous wall of street art at the corner of rue Barrault and rue Alphand, dedicated to the creation of pictographic street art ↓

The wild artwork on Passage Boiton and rue Buot
↓

WELCOME
to Asia !

Butte-aux-Cailles is bursting with Asian shops, where you can travel without leaving the capital. Supermarkets offer sweets and drinks in unusual flavors, not to mention all kinds of exotic fruits. Above all, prepare to discover delicious surprises at its restaurants.

INVENTIVE FLORAL TEAS AND TISANES AT L'EMPIRE DES THÉS

101 avenue d'Ivry, Paris 13th

PERFECTLY FLUFFY CAKES AT LA PÂTISSERIE DE CHOISY

62 avenue de Choisy, Paris 13th

THE TASTIEST JAPANESE TARTS IN THE CAPITAL AT PABLO CHEESE TART

128 rue de Tolbiac, Paris 13th

LUSCIOUS VIETNAMESE SOUPS AT PHO BIDA

36-38 rue Nationale, Paris 13th

TANG FRÈRES SUPERMARKETS FOR SPICES, GYOZA, AND BAO AT FRIENDLY PRICES

48 avenue d'Ivry and 168 avenue de Choisy, Paris 13th

THE MOST HISTORIC CHINESE RESTAURANT IN PARIS, CHINATOWN OLYMPIADE

44 avenue d'Ivry, Paris 13th

THE BEST RAMEN IN THE CAPITAL AT LA TABLE DU LAMEN

72 avenue de Choisy, Paris 13th

GORGEOUS TABLEWARE AND FRESH FOOD AND PRODUCE AT PARIS STORE

44 avenue d'Ivry, Paris 13th

HOTELS WE ADORE

HÔTEL HENRIETTE
FOR A ROMANTIC NIGHT

When a former fashion editor opens her own hotel, it's practically a guarantee that it will be very well-decorated. Flowered wallpaper, lovely vintage furniture, and a winter garden reminiscent of *Alice in Wonderland*. After having shared some tapas, we love to set down our bags for a romantic evening. Our favorite room? Number 22, where the floral wallpaper makes you feel like you're sleeping in a country house.

9 rue des Gobelins, Paris 13th. Deluxe double room from €149. Cheese plate €12. Tzatziki €5.

Hôtel Henriette / © Hôtel Henriette Rive Gauche

C.O.Q HÔTEL
FOR WORKING REMOTELY

Poke your head into this trendy, always-open "squatter's" hotel, which has the (rare!) option of **reserving a room for just a few hours.** Not ready for an afternoon of debauchery? Set yourself up instead in the coworking space, open from 10:30 a.m. to 6:30 p.m., which is perfect for working and networking. The perfect touch? The unlimited drinks option.

15 rue Edouard Manet, Paris 13th. €15 day rate with unlimited drinks.

Coq Hôtel / © C.O.Q Hôtel

Piscine de la Butte-aux-Cailles / © Emanuela Cino

WE'D CROSS PARIS FOR...
BUTTE-AUX-CAILLES SWIMMING POOL

A place where movies have been filmed (Arnaud Desplechin and Gilles Lellouche have incidentally shot scenes here), this 1924 architectural gem offers a 108-foot indoor pool under the arches, which makes it **feel like you're in an aquatic cathedral.** Unique in its class in Paris: the outdoor pool, heated to 82°F, is open year-round. Go for a tan in summer and a Nordic bath in winter!

5 place Paul Verlaine, Paris 13th. Admission €3.50.

Chic Shopping

Pépins et trognons / © Simon Amouyel

PÉPINS ET TROGNONS

The brainchild of two friends, this cute boutique offers a selection of **vintage, French, and eco-friendly products** to help you reduce waste throughout your home. You'll find a selection of bath products, French games that don't break, and other indestructible utensils, all at way more affordable prices than in most "organic" establishments.

111 boulevard Auguste Blanqui, Paris 13th. Two-toned 1970s carafe €19.90.

SOLLA

In this incredibly cool **eat-in grocery concept store,** you can fill your basket with fresh seasonal products sourced less than ninety-three miles from Paris. But there's more! It's most lovable feature? A pocket-size eatery where owner Béa turns out divine sandwiches, quiches, tarts, and cookies, lovingly prepared and at unbeatable prices. Special nod to the Saturday brunch!

26 rue Duméril, Paris 13th. Prix fixe menus €9.80 and €14.80. Brunch €18.

MY FAVORITES

DO IT IN PARIS

MY FAVORITES

IDYLLIC
STROLLS

Parc Montsouris / © Emanuela Cino

La petite alsace / © Emanuela Cino

Cité florale / © Emanuela Cino

PARC MONTSOURIS

Built under Napoleon III (who was inspired by the London parks famous for their vast stretches of lawn), this romantic and verdant **thirty-seven-acre English garden** is the ideal spot to have a casual picnic.

Main entry at 2 rue Gazan, Paris 14th.

LA PETITE ALSACE – LA PETITE RUSSIE

Descend Butte-aux-Cailles and stop at 10 rue Daviel to discover all **the lovely Alsatian houses.** Further down, 22 rue Barrault is home to the discreet Little Russia: a curious line of white homes that was once reserved for (primarily Russian) taxi drivers.

10 rue Daviel, Paris 13th.

LA CITÉ FLORALE

An island of green filled with **life-size dollhouses,** each with its own garden. We love to get lost along the streets lined with mimosa trees, wisteria, and iris, deeply inhaling the scent of the flowers so skillfully maintained by the residents.

Between rues Boussingault, Brillat-Savarin, and Auguste Lançon, Paris 13th.

Canal Saint-Martin & République

Stroll the length of the colorful boutiques along the canal, shop for quirky treasures in Little India, or join an impromptu party. Once a working-class neighborhood, the area around canal Saint-Martin is bursting with vibrant, supertrendy spots, from rue de Marseille to République, passing through avenue Parmentier along the way.

10th & 11th Arrondissements

Clara Caggini

Gros Bao / © Emanuela Cino

GROS BAO

A canal mainstay, this **enormous Chinese eatery** cofounded by Céline Chung and Billy Pham is a must for lovers of street food and Hong Kong. Signature dishes include crispy spring rolls, pork and ginger bao, and even a jumbo Peking duck to share that requires three days' preparation. Wash it all down with a spicy cocktail.

72 quai de Jemmapes, Paris 10th.
Two pork buns €8.50.

LES RÉSISTANTS

Committed to the slow food movement, this restaurant brings together the most responsible French producers, with a short, of-the-moment menu that changes each day depending on what comes in. You might find charcuterie and cheese boards to start, beef ravioli, and a classic whipped-cream-topped tarte tatin, all to be savored in the country house setting. Psst: poke your head into the ridiculously good grocery and wine cellar at number 29 on the same street.

16–18 rue du Château d'Eau, Paris 10th.
Prix fixe lunch €24.

CAFÉ LES DEUX GARES

This **authentic train station bistro** comes to life at 7 a.m., when you can have a comforting coffee and croissant, and stays open through the evening so you can satisfy your hankering for a glass of wine and a plate of saucisson. Jonathan Schweizer (formerly of Sauvage) provides satisfying twists on regional dishes, from oysters to foie gras, not to mention blood sausage. And to wash it all down, there are amazing bottles of natural and biodynamic wines.

1 rue des Deux Gares, Paris 10th. Blood sausage €27.

GÉOSMINE

Chef Maxime Bouttier presents **exuberant, colorful dishes** in which regional cuisine gets the special-night-out treatment in a hip foodie setting. The result? Bold pairings like crispy meatball-style rillette amuse-bouches, along with delicate eel and flower tartelettes. As your curiosity is piqued with long-forgotten dishes like cow's udder (with caviar, s'il vous plait), the sommelier guides you through a food-wine pairing that borders on perfection.

71 rue de la Folie Méricourt, Paris 11th. Eight-course tasting menu €109.

EARLY JUNE

Created by Camille Machet and Victor Vautier, **this always-full, cool, industrial-style wine bar** stays true to the neighborhood's vibe. Chefs from around the world come to take up residency in the kitchen, turning out impeccably sourced, extremely fresh products prepared with panache. Added bonus? The wine cellar offers a great selection of natural wines, which can be ordered for the table or to take back home.

19 rue Jean Poulmarch, Paris 10th. Cocktail of the day €8.

BICHETTES

This is the rare gem that checks all the boxes: comforting food, vin orange, vegetarian options, charming service, a little terrace that's perfect for sipping an aperitif, and Insta-friendly decor. In short, a bistro where you can have a good time without the trap of a lengthy menu. The focus is on the bestsellers on the chalkboard, which change with the weeks and seasons: breaded red squid with chorizo, melted Comté cheese with honey and thyme, or a rustic tart of the day.

11 rue Marie et Louise, Paris 10th. Seasonal tart €18.

GRAND CAFÉ D'ATHÈNES

A Paris–Athens run that only requires the metro. This bistro headed up by Chloé Monchalin has everything you'd want: homey dishes to be shared in a decor that looks like a vacation home. We're loving the bifktekia with beef and tomatoes, the most tender we've tasted, which you can enjoy in a pita to go. Grilled halloumi, salads, and French fries with feta are also on the menu, in unexpected renditions that can be shared—or not.

74 rue du Faubourg Saint-Denis, Paris 10th. Prix fixe lunch €25.

Grand Café d'Athènes / © Sophia van den Hoek

MY FAVORITES

Do IT IN
PARIS

MY FAVORITES

HÔTEL GRAND AMOUR

TO SEE AND BE SEEN

A mainstay of high-society Paris! Known for welcoming throngs of VIPs and models, who gather to clink glasses every fashion week, the hotel's Book Bar has proven to be the trendy hot spot to dance, have a drink, and grab a bite before heading over to the capital's hip nightclubs. As for the food, the brunch served on the patio is an absolute must. Menus are updated as various trendsetting chefs do their residencies.

18 rue de la Fidélité, Paris 10th.
Red Chili Cocktail €15.

Hôtel Grand Amour © Hôtel Grand Amour

TWO
UNIQUE
COFFEE SHOPS

BUDDY BUDDY
THE MOST GOURMET

It's the new coffee shop in the neighborhood, straight off the boat from Brussels. The specialty? The hazelnut, almond, and peanut butters used in its signature gourmet drinks and foodporn-worthy cookies. Special nod to the decor, which is completely Instagrammable and a touch futuristic. Our advice? Since it's often packed on the weekends, order to go and take advantage of one of the beautiful sunny patches of green alongside the canal.
15 rue de Marseille, Paris 10th.
Buddy signature coffee €5.50.

BONJOUR JACOB
THE BRAINIEST

You might think you're in Berlin in this new café, which features one room and two different settings. While young professionals frenetically type on their laptops in between glugs of excellent coffee, other customers flip through the latest magazines and fashion or design books in the library section up front. After you've dipped some of your carrot cake into an iced mocha, grab the latest copy of *Mastermind* and some lovely books to decorate your coffee table on your way out.
28 rue Yves Toudic, Paris 10th.
Matcha latte €5.

Buddy buddy / © Rotsoina / Latte in Paris

Everything You Need to Celebrate Your Home Sweet Home

Landline / © Olivia Tran

LANDLINE

This **chic, eco-friendly drugstore,** which looks just like an old-fashioned bric-a-brac shop, makes you need things you never suspected you would. Items on offer include household design and fashion objects, gardening tools, stylish children's games, and even French beauty labels. Rummaging has never been so sexy! Here you're not just buying organic and eco-friendly, but, above all, beautiful, collectible, authentic, and sustainable items, ranging from feather dusters to fluffy throw blankets, and even a perfectly kitschy duck-shaped carafe.

*107 avenue Parmentier, Paris 11*th.
Coconut fiber sponge €3.50.

POMPON BAZAR

Specializing in handwoven artisanal decor, in particular beautiful Berber and Kilim rugs, this concept store promises **a voyage to the other side of the Mediterranean** along the Silk and Spice Roads. And that's not all: you can also find wicker baskets, checkered babouche slippers, pretty bouquets of dried flowers, and even candles and wax sachets encrusted with botanical plants. It's perfect for dreamers on the hunt for rustic decor.

*10 rue de Lancry, Paris 10*th.
Large Berber rug approximately €500.

MOUSTACHE

Design lovers and collectors of unique pieces won't know where to start at the Moustache publishing house, which chose this vibrant neighborhood to exhibit and sell its treasures. Inside, you'll find **the best of designer furniture** and decor objects that are both fun and desirable. The playful will adore the Bold chairs, trendy Zodiac mirrors by Jean-Baptiste Fastrez, or Ionna Vautrin TGV lamps.

*17 rue Beaurepaire, Paris 10*th.
TGV lamps €350.

RÉTROFUTUR

The concept? Shop for cutting-edge designer speakers at accessible prices. This high-tech concept store, opened by a group of friends who are passionate about sound, offers a selection of high-quality audio products. You'll find retro gems like 1960s speakers from the French brand Elipson, audiovisual furniture from La Boîte Concept, and even Cambridge all-in-one players.

*55 quai de Valmy, Paris 10*th.
Elipson Planet M Subwoofer €549.

LA TRÉSORERIE

This **Ali Baba's cave of Scandinavian fashion** has taken residence on a cobblestoned street in the trendy 10th, offering lovely, eco-friendly, and thoughtfully designed products. Otherwise known as the art of making buying a broom cool. Here you'll find it all, from pretty brushes and other trendy accessories to do your cleaning with, little stools, and stunning coffee tables, ceramic tableware, stylish paintings, and cute bathroom accessories.

11 rue du Château d'Eau, Paris 10th.
Linen cloth napkin €13.

PLANTES POUR TOUS

Bolstered by the success of its flash sales at pop-up stores, Plantes Pour Tous has decamped alongside the canal this year, with an oversize boutique where you can **shop for plants at superlow prices** year-round. There are plenty of miniature cacti, tropical plants, and bouquets of dried flowers, not to mention its many vases, colorful planters, wicker baskets, and 1980s candlesticks.

13 rue Jean Poulmarch, Paris 10th.
Bouquet of dried flowers €25.

ARTAZART

This amazing gallery, filled with **art and design works,** never disappoints. In addition to art exhibitions, this canal-side bookstore offers a selection of books signed by buzz-generating authors and cutting-edge magazines like *Purple Magazine*, *Muse Magazine*, or *Self Service*. Cool bonus: the stationery area has artsy, supercolorful posters.

83 quai de Valmy, Paris 10th. Artsy poster €35.

La trésorerie / © Molly Seyes

TWO SPOTS
FOR SELF-CARE

ABSOLUTION

This superbusy beauty salon frequented by fashion editors and television personalities goes all in on organics so you can **relax and renew naturally.** On the menu: custom treatments, SOS masks for damaged skin, and even workshop and office spaces. We love signature products like a brightening body scrub you can slip into your suitcase or the Beau Jour cream, designed to be mixed with your own serum to boost its antiaging effectiveness.

30 rue des Vinaigriers, Paris 10th.
One-hour signature treatment €100.

LA MONTGOLFIÈRE

You don't need to be a gym rat to belong to this **glamorous athletic club.** More than a gym, Montgolfière is a true gathering place. In addition to its weight room, cardio equipment, classes, and sauna and steam room (there are also massage treatment rooms, naturally), members have access to a coworking space with comfy couches and a library, as well as an eatery run by Season, which offers excellent casual bites like acai bowls, well-balanced salads, and detoxifying juices.

25 rue Yves Toudic, Paris 10th.
Monthly subscription €179.

Centre commercial / © Centre Commercial

WE LOVE...

CENTRE COMMERCIAL

At this **of-the-moment concept store** dreamed up by the founders of Veja sneakers, everything is eco-friendly. You'll find young French designers (Umlaut, Justine Clenquet, Vaillant), stylish Aeyde or Miista shoes, and even great beauty products like the ones from Talm for pregnant women. And for cool parents, the same savvy curating can be found just down the street at the dedicated children's boutique.

2 rue de Marseille and 22 rue Yves Toudic, Paris 10th. Birkenstock sandals €110.

Du pain et des idées / © Emanuela Cino

DU PAIN ET DES IDÉES

Hidden inside this authentic Second Empire space is **one of the best bakeries in the capital.** And that's an understatement! Here the bread is baked on a stone like they did in the old days, resulting in a perfectly cooked loaf with a thick, crispy crust. It must be said that Christophe Vasseur is not content with making mere baguettes. We line up for his Pain des Amis and for his oversize orange blossom–flavored brioche. His other signature bake? The Escargot, a morning pastry that resembles a pain au raisin but is filled with pistachio and chocolate, or house-made pralines. Too good.

34 rue Yves Toudic, Paris 10th.
Pistachio escargot €3.95.

MY FAVORITES

DO IT IN PARIS

MY FAVORITES

PASSAGE BRADY
nº 1 à 6

43   43

BOLLYWOOD
in Paris!

5 SPOTS for traveling to India with your commuter pass

THULASI

Anyone who loves natural products will adore this small ayurvedic herbal shop, which carries excellent oils for body, massage, and hair.

58 passage Brady, Paris 10ᵗʰ.

PASSAGE BRADY

The scents of spices and incense emanate the length of this discreet covered passageway, which is home to boutiques and restaurants.

*33 boulevard de Strasbourg —
46 rue du Faubourg-Saint-Denis, Paris 10ᵗʰ.*

SAREE PALACE

A tiny paradise where you can dress up like an Indian princess. Choose from among the numerous embroidered saris, and other sparkling accessories.

*182 rue du Faubourg-
Saint-Denis,
Paris 10ᵗʰ.*

VELAN

A grocery store where you can shop for all the Indian essentials: rose syrups, incense, candles, teas, and chutneys.

87-88 passage Brady, Paris 10ᵗʰ.

BARANAAN

Embark immediately for Mumbai at this speakeasy-inspired cocktail bar. The rose cocktail is delicious paired with a gigantic dish of naan and tender butter chicken.

*7 rue du Faubourg-Saint-Martin,
Paris 10ᵗʰ.*

ÉLYSÉE, ÉTOILE & TERNES

From the Triangle d'Or to Ternes, all the way to Parc Monceau, the chicest section of Paris moves to the rhythm of the stars! We are, of course, thinking of its iconic square (which spans twelve sublime avenues), but also of its luxury hotels and Michelin-starred restaurants. Tight budget? Skip this section!

Clémence Renoux

Enni Udon. © Guillaume Czerw

ENNI UDON

At **this chic izakaya-inspired canteen,** we order noodles (hot or cold), to be dipped in broth (or not), and slurped down with wooden chopsticks and a spoon. The star items on the menu include the Tempura Udon, which comes in a hot dashi broth made from fish, kombu, and shitake mushrooms. You immerse pieces of shrimp in the soup, one by one, so they maintain their crispiness. Also worth ordering: the ultracrunchy karaage, katsudon, and, for dessert, the must-have house-made dorayaki.

6 rue de la Renaissance, Paris 8th. Tempura Udon €21.

CÈNA

Diners come from far and wide to try out the colorful, refined cooking of young Japanese chef Hideki Nakamura. We put ourselves completely in Nakamura's hands here, ordering one of **the chef's choice menus.** The four-course Discovery menu is more than sufficient: enticing amuse-bouches, langoustine with strawberries and horseradish cream, tasty veal and green asparagus, and a kawaii rhubarb dessert. The dishes change as the chef sees fit, depending on the season and what comes in from the market. An extra benefit: the selection of natural wines, such as an excellent Burgundy Aligoté with a far-out label or a perfect Oxymoron vin orange. An absolute must-try!

23 rue Treilhard, Paris 8th. Four-course lunch €75.

VIVE

The most powerful duo in cooking, David and Stéphanie Le Quellec, are back with a project focused on the ingredient the pair loves most—seafood. Our advice? Ask to sit at the bar so you can admire the chef as he manages the garde-manger team, while a beautiful tuna aging in the glass case holds court. We share amberjack with chimichurri sauce, rockfish soup, and the menu's must-try dish: **the sexiest octopus in Paris,** which arrives enveloped in a divine creamy harissa sauce.

62 avenue des Ternes, Paris 17th. Half octopus €59.

LA LORRAINE

Anyone who has never tasted one of La Lorraine's **gargantuan seafood platters** is not 100 percent Parisian. This legendary brasserie, sister restaurant to L'Alsace on the Champs-Élysées, is without peer for those seeking an age-old restaurant where you can rub shoulders with western Paris's upper crust as they rip apart their lobsters. What's more, Laura Gonzalez has created an extraordinary setting with carpets, mosaics, and murals. You'll think you're in a movie. It's the art of combining anachronistic elegance with the taste of the moment. Note: all shellfish are available for delivery.

2 place des Ternes, Paris 17th. Oyster Sheller seafood platter €46.

THREE MICHELIN-STARRED MENUS FOR LESS THAN €80

Il Carpaccio / © Zoé Fidji

A tip for the budget-conscious: take the afternoon off and have lunch at one of these breathtaking Michelin-starred restaurants.

IL CARPACCIO

This Michelin-starred Italian restaurant, located in the Royal Monceau-Raffles Paris hotel, never disappoints. Chef duo Alessandra Del Favero and Oliver Piras are at the helm, offering light and modern dishes that highlight the best Italian regional specialties. The pastas are clearly worth the detour: Da Vittorio paccheri with tomatoes and basil, the signature tagliolini with truffles, and the perfectly crunchy "Elephant ear" Milanese cutlet.
37 avenue Hoche, Paris 8th.
Prix fixe lunch €70.

PAVYLLON

Yannick Alléno, owner of Pavillon Ledoyen, is the man behind this gourmet bistro spot (which now holds one Michelin star), filling a terrible gap between Concorde and Grand Palais. The modern bistro vibe runs throughout the luxurious, contemporary space dreamed up by renowned interior designer Chahan Minassian. Want an excellent idea? Go for the three-course prix fixe lunch, which might include the now-cultish Obsiblue shrimp cocktail, red mullet, and wild strawberries paired with an orange blossom cream. Divine!
8 avenue Dutuit, Paris 8th. Prix fixe lunch €78.

HELEN

Hidden on an unassuming street close to the Place de l'Étoile, Chef Sébastien Carmona-Porto's Michelin-starred restaurant gives pride of place to exceptional fish dishes, offering an unbeatable price-quality ratio. A favorite haunt of the neighborhood's politicos, we too delight in its wonders, sourced from small fishing boats and often served in raw preparations: sea bass carpaccio, langoustine tails, sea bream ceviche. Given that refinement is the only guiding principle, it's not surprising that some regulars come multiple times a week!
3 rue Berryer, Paris 8th. Prix fixe lunch €52.

Festive Dinners

Gala / © Helen Karam

transports you to the heart of Marrakech—with neither passport nor suitcase required. Not to mention there are musicians playing their ouds and violins, belly dancers undulating between the tables, and DJs who rock the house, keeping the room on its feet until 2 a.m.

On the table: hummus in three colors, lamb skewers, chicken tagine.

6 rue Arsène Houssaye, Paris 8th. Brochettes de kefta €24.

BŒUF SUR LE TOIT

The cult spot from the roaring twenties where Christian Dior, Brigitte Bardot, and Yves Saint Laurent used to dance had fallen off our radar. Since Patrick Bruel and Benjamin Patou took it over, it has regained its rightful place as **a celebrity haunt**. Chic stars and fashion gangs tumble through the door at this incredibly glam restaurant. Built like a music hall with decor by Alexis Mabille, the space features a grand piano, antique mirrored tables, crystal lamps, and patterned rugs.

On the table: macaroni with morels, tartare with shoestring fries, seafood platters.

34 rue du Colisée, Paris 8th. Tartare €28.

MONDAINE DE PARISO

With its neo-cabaret vibe, the former Roxie really shows its stuff: wall-to-wall carpet, animal prints (leopard leads the pack), sexy mirrors, and gossip-inducing canopy beds. Play the field on both floors, which include a bar, alcoves, a library, and smoking room, where you can roam freely and **toast to new acquaintances**. Each "fête" features musicians and singers, who play the nostalgia card with French variety and global hits everyone knows by heart—everyone can happily sing along! On the table: haricot verts and mushrooms, octopus with new potatoes, linguine with truffles.

23 rue de Ponthieu, Paris 8th. Lobster roll €29.

GIGI

After Ramatuelle and Val d'Isère, Laurent de Gourcuff (Paris Society) has now opened a festive "vacation" restaurant in Paris, to the

A trendy nighthawk stronghold, the 8th is not lacking in sceney dinner spots! Note: you'll definitely need to make reservations.

GALA

It's the festive Middle Eastern restaurant we were waiting for in Paris! With its opulent, luxurious palace-style decor, featuring hanging feather chandeliers, colorful stained glass, velvety fabrics, and a Bedouin tent hiding an enormous table, Gala elegantly reinvents the genre and immediately great joy of his stylish regulars. He needed a spot worthy of the name for his VIP clientele. He found it on **the top floor of the Théâtre des Champs-Élysées**, which boasts a mind-boggling view and two terraces that get everything right. There's even an incredible orchestra that primes the scene for wild nights. It goes without saying that the models and beautiful people flow in every evening. On the table: sea bass with stracciatella, vitello tonnato, truffled arancini.

15 avenue Montaigne, Paris 8ᵗʰ. Spritz €17.

GIULIA

All is well! A few feet from the Champs-Élysées, the great tastes of Italy have taken up residence in **this music-focused restaurant, set to the rhythm of live music and DJ sets.** Giulia's sweet, cozy interior features lots of carpeting, idyllic wallpaper, and inviting velvet banquettes. This "beauty of the night" opens its arms wide to groups of friends celebrating a night out, welcoming them in complete comfort to the enormous space filled with alcoves and a mixed soundtrack of Italian songs and all-time hits you can't help humming along to!

On the table: pappardelle al ragù, beef tenderloin with roasted potatoes, tiramisu.

20 rue Quentin Bauchart, Paris 8ᵗʰ. Vitello tonnato €32.

Mondaine de Pariso / © Romain Ricard

CHIC DRINKS

THE BEST COCKTAILS *of the Golden Triangle are over here!*

SIR WINSTON

In a setting that evokes the Orient Express, sample excellent Indian-influenced potions, such as Kesar with saffron gin, bergamot liqueur, fresh lemon juice, cardamom syrup, and cranberry nectar.

5 rue de Presbourg, Paris 16ᵗʰ. Signature cocktails €14 to €16.

MONSIEUR GEORGE

We love **the bar in this five-star hotel**, with all its green Zellige tiles and mirrors. It's the perfect place to impress your date with a fruity Chequer cocktail featuring cognac, pear puree, orgeat syrup, and egg white.

17 rue Washington, Paris 8ᵗʰ. Signature cocktails €23.

MUN

A high rooftop perched over the Champs-Élysées where you can socialize while raising a glass of refined elixirs, like the Kuro Tsuki featuring smoked tea vodka, lychee juice, black lemon syrup, and black sesame.

52 avenue des Champs-Élysées, Paris 8ᵗʰ. Cocktails €18 to €22.

FASHION

HEADQUARTERS

KITH

Over the past ten years, Kith has become **the "It" brand for fans of American-style bling.** It must be said that its founder, Ronnie Fieg, marketing king and New York street culture insider, is one of the most influential entrepreneurs on the East Coast, idolized by nearly a million followers. The three floors provide a mix of fashion, culture, and decor, along with an outpost of New York cult eatery Sadelle's, where you can enjoy brunch with an indoor Parisian café vibe.

WHAT'S THERE?

A very soft sweatsuit, a jean jacket embroidered with the brand's name, a Kaws teddy bear, cutting-edge books on photography or skate culture, a vintage Chanel or Vuitton bag and, of course, swoon-worthy sneakers.
49 rue Pierre Charron, Paris 8th. Nike Air Jordan low-tops €120.

MODES

Paris needed a new spot capable of generating **Colette-level fashion obsession.** A store where the collections were *that* fashion-forward, chic, and fun. It's a done deal with the first French outpost of Modes, the Italian concept store already drawing crowds in cities like Milan, Porto Cervo, and Portofino. The result? An amazing two-level space (the blue lagoon staircase is gorgeous) where the minimalist interior brings out the bold colors of the men's and women's accessories.

WHAT'S THERE?

A Vetements blazer, Jacquemus bags, a Paco Rabanne metallic top, incredibly hip T-shirts from the new Modes Garments line, a Courrèges jacket, Birkenstocks, a sexy Rick Owens dress, and sneakers curated by StockX.
17 rue François Ier, Paris 8th. Modes Garments T-shirt €145.

MONOGRAM

It's collective hysteria at the Place de l'Étoile. This **secondhand luxury goods specialist** recently opened its first boutique just a few steps (actually twelve) from the Arc de Triomphe. The vibe is pop, the playlist is funky, and there are "It" bags galore. It's a slice of heaven for fashionistas who swear by Chanel, Gucci, and Saint Laurent, in a superfun setting: think wallets dispensed from a vending machine, colorful bags in Barbie pink cubbies, and mannequins with fluorescent wigs. Also noteworthy: the repair service, estimates provided upon request.

WHAT'S THERE?

Celine glasses, Dior necklaces and belts, Hermès home items, a Gucci cardigan, Chanel bags in every color, even a Fendi denim Baguette bag.
12-14 avenue Victor Hugo, Paris 16th. Chloé sandals €250.

Monogram / © Monogram Paris

MUSEUMS TO DISCOVER

MUSÉE NISSIM DE CAMONDO

At the end of Parc Monceau, this extraordinary, dignified museum contains a multitude of French treasures collected by Moïse de Camondo, including furniture, paintings, porcelain, rugs, tapestries, and gold and silver jewelry dating back to the eighteenth century. It's truly **a trip back in time!**

*63 rue de Monceau, Paris 8*th*.*
Full-price admission €12.

MUSÉE CERNUSCHI

Located just behind the Camondo, **this stunning museum specializing in Asian art** offers an extremely rare collection of pieces from China and Japan that belonged to Italian patriot Henri Cernuschi. Get ready for an incredibly inspiring journey through this former residence, where you'll discover masterpieces like unspeakably beautiful Buddhas, wooden tigers, porcelain, and engravings.

*7 avenue Velasquez, Paris 8*th*.*
Free admission.

MUSÉE JACQUEMART-ANDRÉ

Looking at the austere facade, you'd never suspect there's an awe-inspiring courtyard containing **an architectural jewel, complete with a winter garden** and an imposing, quintessentially Second Empire staircase. Better yet, after an exhibition, grab a spot at the tearoom and enjoy a steaming hot Sencha tea and a yummy pastry.

*158 boulevard Haussmann, Paris 8*th*.*
Full-price admission €17.

PETIT PALAIS

We're (re)discovering this younger sibling opposite the Grand Palais. The building, which was also designed for the 1900 Paris Exposition, is especially beautiful. We spent so many hours roaming around the vestibule, the large galleries, the pavilions, and the garden that we almost forgot to admire the works on display in the current exhibition!

*Avenue Winston Churchill, Paris 8*th*.*
Full-price admission €15.

A PICNIC
AT PARC MONCEAU

The majestic entrance provides the promise of a royal promenade! Dating back to the eighteenth century, the magnificent Parc Monceau is the perfect place for **a romantic stroll through nature** before having a picnic on the soft grass opposite the Renaissance-style arcade, the rotunda, or the waterfall.

THE BEST SNACK RIGHT BEFORE YOU GO?

A salad, pâté en croûte, or grilled cheese with truffles from **MAM** (*22 rue Fourcroy, Paris 17*th*), the yummiest take-out spot in the neighborhood. All you need to complete the *Alice in Wonderland* vibe is put down your blanket and a few flowers.

*35 boulevard de Courcelles, Paris 8*th*.*
Free admission.

Grands Boulevards & Opéra

Historically a place for parties and other pleasures, the Grands Boulevards has retained its roguish character. From Bonne Nouvelle to Place de l'Opéra, this vibrant and energetic artery offers a string of cafés, restaurants, bars, theaters, and cinemas, where crowds flock both day and night. Boredom? Not a chance!

2nd & 9th Arrondissements

Sandra Serpero

SOMETHING SWEET

MOMZI

The Rolls-Royce of doughnuts,
the gold standard of its class! Chef
Raamin Samiyi makes a splash with
light-as-air doughnut specials at one
of the most popular patisseries in the
city. The secrets? A thrice-fermented
sourdough brioche dough and frying
in coconut oil. Of the doughnuts
permanently on offer, we love to dive
into the Mother of Matcha, sprinkled
with Gyokuro green tea leaves and
roasted rice.
1 rue Cherubini, Paris 2ⁿᵈ.
Each item €8 to €10.

JADE GENIN

**In the Genin family, chocolate is
a passion!** Daughter Jade has gone
into pastry and is debuting her first
collections at this exquisite white-
and-gold boutique. We adore her
tremendously good offerings, like the
adorable Pyramidions with ganache
centers in a feast of flavors, the rochers
(which go down way too easily), and
the absolutely irresistible spreads!
33 avenue de l'Opéra, Paris 2ⁿᵈ.
Mini chocolate bar €3.

Donut Momzi / © Leonardo Denizon

Micho / © Centre Commercial

MICHO

The insanely good sandwich shop from chef Julien Sebbag (Créatures, Tortuga) stokes appetites with original creations stuffed into delicious, extrasoft challah rolls.
48 rue de Richelieu, Paris 1st. Crash Kebab €16.

MOSUGO

Young Michelin-starred chef Mory Sako has mastered the art of fried chicken like no other, and is offering an even naughtier street food version here, in the form of a crazy good burger on pretzel bread, served with sweet potato fries and miso mayo.
35 boulevard Haussmann, Paris 9th.
Slim Menu €21.50.

BAR VENDÔME

The menu at this classic neighborhood bistro rolls out small pleasures to delight, like its delicious and well-stuffed sandwiches, for devouring at the counter or purchasing to go.
8 rue des Capucines, Paris 2nd. Ham with butter €5.50.

A Sandwich on the Fly!

THE (OBLIGATORY!) PASSAGE DES PANORAMAS

A kingdom for foodies, this covered passageway next to the Théâtre des Variétés offers lovers of fine food an assortment of cuisines that will take them on a trip from the Mediterranean to Japan.

OUR ESSENTIAL SPOTS
in the Passage des Panoramas

GYOZA BAR

This tiny Zen-like jewel box makes incredible made-to-order gyoza from its counter.

Eight gyozas + side €10

RACINES

Sardinian chef Simone Tondo runs this ravishing bistro full of charm, turning out exquisite transalpine cuisine that we adore.

Tagliolini al ragù €22

CERTIFIED

A top-notch coffee shop that roasts excellent specialty coffees on-site.

Espresso €2.70

CLUB COCHON

This aptly named spot declares its love for hearty plates, dishing out one of the best sausages with mashed potatoes in Paris!

All-pork pâté en croûte €10

CANARD ET CHAMPAGNE

This stylish restaurant provides a chic spin on regional specialties.

Duck shepherd's pie €14

CAFFÈ STERN

This Starck-decorated high-society Italian bistro offers a menu of elevated Italian classics: cappuccino alla Bolognese, polenta with smoked cod and bottarga, and gnocchi with gorgonzola.

FAGGIO PANORAMAS

Pizzas cooked in a best-in-class wood-burning oven with awesome toppings.

Fior di latte margherita €12

Daily special €20

OUR FAVORITE EATERIES

L'ENTENTE, LE BRITISH BRASSERIE

Located a stone's throw from the Place de l'Opéra, this charming eatery offers **British classics, all made in-house,** right down to the ketchup! Dive into the incredible fish and chips with tartar sauce, and hustle over for the weekend brunch—it's one of the rare places in the capital that does not impose a prix fixe. What a pleasure! Menu essentials include the Full Entente plate (fried eggs, sausage, bacon, baked beans, mushrooms, sautéed potatoes, tomato), which can also be made vegetarian.

13 rue Monsigny, Paris 2nd. Fish & Chips €24.

MORI VENICE BAR

This **fine-dining Italian spot** opposite the stock exchange is certainly the classiest address in the area. Decorated by Philippe Starck, the Mori Venice Bar transports us to the City of Canals with its excellent Venetian cooking. During the day, business lunches reign supreme: the menu even lists a CAC 40 (stock market index) Menu! At night, it draws an elegant Parisian crowd, along with chic internationals (naturally, since the Ritz concierge services recommend it), all eager to taste the incredible fried fish. Last but not least: the trolley of freshly churned ice cream!

27 rue Vivienne, Paris 2nd.
CAC 40 Menu €44. Mains from €38.

BOUILLON CHARTIER

It's **the most popular cheap-eats destination in Paris,** open since 1896. And it's impossible to miss since there's always a crowd in front! Inside, you'll find an art deco room and servers clad in black vests and white aprons darting among the tables and scrawling orders. The menu features traditional cuisine such as terrine, escargots, roast chicken, and crème caramel. It's hard to spend more than €25, wine included.

7 rue du Faubourg Montmartre, Paris 9th.
Dishes from €7.

Bouillon Chartier / © Max Ledieu

BISSAC

This **elegant little bistro,** with its charming terrace nestled under the arcades on rue des Colonnes, satisfies the appetite for chef and master restauranteur Damien Boudier's signature bistro cooking. His specialty? Traditional, seasonally focused food showcasing vegetables (zucchini flower fritters with goat cheese), savory cuts of meat (veal chop with sauce au poivre and house-made fries), and delicious gourmet desserts to top it all off.

10 rue de la Bourse, Paris 2nd.
Mains €20 to €85 for the prime rib for two.

ACCENTS

Japanese pastry chef Ayumi Sugiyama has teamed up with her husband, chef Romain Mahi, at this Michelin-starred restaurant. The pair offers **a fine-dining experience that is French, yet open to other cuisines.** The four-, six-, or seven-course prix fixe menus include incredibly delicate dishes that flow between land and sea, along with signature wow-inducing desserts like the Sugar Bubble or the extraordinary, light-as-a-feather Chiffon Cake.

24 rue Feydeau, Paris 2nd. Prix fixe menus from €52.

AU PETIT RICHE

With its **ragamuffin spirit,** old-school service, and traditional French cuisine, Le Petit Riche has all the charm of the old-fashioned bistros we adore, but with a wine bar and formidable cellar containing over five thousand bottles! We love sitting down for an aperitif with friends and snacking on a cheese plate, pâté en croûte, and a few glasses of Saumur Champigny or Sancerre. Bonuses: a supercute terrace and four private rooms upstairs.

25 rue Le Peletier, Paris 9th. Mains €18 to €35.

MONBLEU

The **classy cheese bar** of the Grands Boulevards! In its beautiful, meticulously decorated dining room, Monbleu offers its topnotch cheese menu, which contains more than eighty selections (Comté, Beaufort, Saint-Nectaire, Tomme des Aravis, juniper-smoked Petit Chèvre) handpicked by Pierre Gay, who holds the title of *Meilleur Ouvrier de France.* Whether you go for lunch or once night falls, we adore the oeufs mi mayo-mimolette, burratina with heirloom tomatoes and cucumber cream, and the devilishly good camembert with white wine and thyme, served warm: yum!

37 rue du Faubourg Montmartre, Paris 9th.
Prix fixe lunch from €19.

AUX LYONNAIS

Alain Ducasse took over this **typical Parisian *bouchon* (traditional bistro) dedicated to Lyonnais cuisine** in 2002. The 100 percent Lyonnais chef Victoria Boller treats us to comforting dishes with an excellent modern spin: quenelles, pork in all its forms, and pâté en croûte. The best option: the Sunday-only *mâchon* menu, where Lyonnais specialties and good wine guarantee a great time.

32 rue Saint-Marc, Paris 2nd. Menu Mâchon €55.

Aux Lyonnais / © Bertille Chabrolle

TEAM ELECTRONICA?
MORE INTO CLASSICAL?

Le Grand Rex, the enormous movie theater and legendary club, has pride of place on boulevard Poissonière. It draws a million visitors, gets the best sneak previews, and is the biggest movie theater in Europe. If Le Grand Rex is the king of cinema, its adjacent club is Paris's temple of techno. All the greatest DJs have lit up its dance floor: Laurent Garnier, Jeff Miles, Carl Cox, Daft Punk, and Justice. In 2023, the Rex Club celebrated its thirty-fifth birthday and got its first facelift! So come meet your friends and dance all night in a brand-new club!

1 boulevard Poissonnière, Paris 2ⁿᵈ.
Rex Club admission €20.

Another monument to culture, with a beauty you'd sell your soul for and a fascinatingly rich history, sits on the square that bears its name: **the Opéra Garnier.** Just visiting it is a show, that's how much the rooms and ceilings enchant with their beauty. As far as the stage goes, the Opéra Garnier owes its renown to excellent programming—it hosts the most important ballets and operas in the world. Everyone should see a performance here at least once in their lives.

Place de l'Opéra, Paris 9ᵗʰ.
Self-guided tour €15.

THE BEST
SPOTS

TO HAVE
A DRINK (OR TWO!)

LE ROUGE À LÈVRES

We love this wine and tapas bar for its boss, the lovely Serge Ahovey (La Mangerie), who knows how to host and has a gift for creating ambiance. It's to him that we owe this **perfectly chill girls'-night-out spot,** which features a tropic-cool decor inspired by his trips to Bali. Le Rouge à Lèvres also has a splendid affordable wine menu with around one hundred excellent options, along with funky share plates to enjoy between rounds of drinks: truffled gouda, Galician beef Cecina, and tataki. A great evening is guaranteed.

6 rue Rougemont, Paris 9th. Wines by the glass €8.50 to €12, bottles from €38.

HARRY'S BAR

Not only is Harry's Bar **the oldest cocktail bar in Europe** (open since 1911), but many legendary recipes were created within its walls: the Bloody Mary was born here! To say there are some jostling at the bar is a nice euphemism, and finding a place is often tough. Want a tip? Come at 7 p.m. sharp and slide into the room downstairs. Leisurely sip a short or tall drink while waiting for 10 p.m., when the musicians settle in—then let the jazz wash over you. After all, George Gershwin composed *An American in Paris* here. Hunger pangs? Order the hot dog!

5 rue Daunou, Paris 2nd. Bloody Mary €15.

THE SHED AT THE HÔTEL DES GRANDS BOULEVARDS

Well hidden on the roof of the Hôtel des Grands Boulevards, **this rooftop is a little haven of peace** that offers not only the obvious panoramic view of the city but also the pleasure of being away from the asphalt. With its unusual U-shape, this intimate refuge balances good sound, effective cocktails by the Experimental Group, and charming little bites: Italian charcuterie, burrata, trout gravlax, and more. It's always a good option.

17 boulevard Poissonnière, Paris 2nd.
Nonalcoholic cocktails €10 and alcoholic cocktails €16.

Harry's bar / © Harry's bar

MY FAVORITES

DO IT IN PARIS

MY FAVORITES

Hôtel Drouot / © Thomas O'Brien

HOW TO INFILTRATE

DROUOT?

In truth, there's nothing simpler! No need to register to take advantage of sales of luxury clothing, high-end jewelry, or exceptional pieces; you need only show up—admission is free. The sole imperatives? Just have your ID and credit card on you—that's all! The Hôtel Drouot contains fifteen sales rooms distributed over three levels. Room 9 on the mezzanine is the prettiest and most iconic; that's where the special sales are held, as well as the exhibitions (there are three or four a year). **Furniture, antiques, paintings, jewelry**—you'll find them all here, even low-priced treasures!

9 rue Drouot, Paris 9ᵗʰ.
Antique earrings €100.

3 SUPERB

THEATERS

TO NAME DROP

THÉÂTRE NATIONAL DE L'OPÉRA-COMIQUE

This theater, which has been around for over three hundred years, boasts **a remarkable palace-style decor,** which by itself is worth the detour. Its programming delights both opera buffs and novices enamored by this unique lyrical genre. What's more, this is where Georges Bizet created his masterpiece, *Carmen* and performed its premier on March 3, 1875.
1 place Boieldieu, Paris 2nd.
Tickets €6 to €149.

Théâtre Edouard VII / © Bernard Richebei

THÉÂTRE EDOUARD VII

Welcome to Théâtre Edouard VII, the English-language theater that became famous after Sacha Guitry declared his love for it for ten years running. The boulevard lies in its soul! Created during the Belle Époque and **built by the king of England** on a jewel of a square hidden from the bustle of the neighborhood, this theater with an awe-inspiring beauty always hits the mark: the magic begins as soon as the curtain rises!
10 place Edouard VII, Paris 9th.
Tickets €10 to €98.

FOLIES BERGÈRE

Opened in 1869, this legendary stage was **the first music hall to open in Paris.** Joséphine Baker, Dalida, Gabin, and Fernandel immortalized it, as did novelists and painters such as Zola in *Nana* or even Manet in his famous painting *A Bar at the Folies-Bergère*. The magic continues in the twenty-first century, with an exhilarating lineup of concerts, shows, and musical comedies guaranteed to thrill.
32 rue Richer, Paris 9th.
Concerts from €20.

INVALIDES, EIFFEL TOWER & MONTPARNASSE

From boulevard Raspail to avenue Rapp, these chic neighborhoods have the biggest concentration of noteworthy monuments and extraordinary museums per square foot. If you love to wander around with no precise destination, your head in the clouds, here are some essential spots for the next time your travels take you to the Left Bank.

7th, 14th & 15th Arrondissements

Pauline de Quatrebarbes

3 MUSEUMS

THAT NEVER

DISSAPOINT

Musée Bourdelle / ©Nicolas Borel et Benoît Fougeirol

MUSÉE BOURDELLE

We often return to this studio-museum dating back to 1878, where we rediscover wonders like sculptures, archives, and photos that transport us to Antoine Bourdelle's time. Take a moment to visit the magnificent gardens and **stroll among the sculptor's works** before sitting down at Rhodia, the museum's restaurant. It offers an incredibly fresh Latin-influenced menu, along with fresh-pressed juices and must-try honey madeleines.
*18 rue Antoine Bourdelle, Paris 15th.
Free admission to permanent collections.*

FONDATION CARTIER POUR L'ART CONTEMPORAIN

This **quintessential exhibition space** is tucked behind a glass facade designed by Jean Nouvel. On view at the foundation: top contemporary artists and exhibitions that often cover uncharted territory. Musicians, illustrators, photographers, designers, and visual artists all take their rightful place in this space, which is always at the cutting edge of current artistic trends. We love to get lost in the immense rooms overlooking the grounds outside, as

we discover the always fascinating works of art.
*261 boulevard Raspail, Paris 14th.
Full-price admission €11.*

MUSÉE RODIN

Dedicated to the sculptor's works, this museum is a must-see for any Beaux Arts fan. You'll come across the artist's most famous works, such as *The Thinker* and *The Gates of Hell*, as well as numerous pieces from his lover, the great artist Camille Claudel. The garden, one of the most incredible in Paris, is home to **outdoor sculptures and hosts evening events, with picnicking** allowed on the grass. With seven magnificent acres open to all, what could be better?
*77 rue de Varenne, Paris 7th.
Admission to museum and gardens €16.*

Musée Rodin / © C. Weiner,
agence photographique musée Rodin

OUR FAVORITE EATERIES

L'AMI JEAN

At **this always lovely bistro,** we sample fine, local cuisine, slavishly following the recommendations of the infallible chef, Stéphane Jégo, who always generously offers tips on how to replicate his cooking methods at home. It must be said that his menu is flawless! It includes whole stuffed turbot cooked three ways, squid a la plancha, and roasted veal chop with garlic and thyme. Underneath the rustic setting lies an ultramodern vision of gastronomy that's revealed as you enjoy the dishes.

27 rue Malar, Paris 7th.
Grilled veal cheek confit €42.

LES DEUX ABEILLES

This is one of our favorite restaurants! **An ultracute tearoom that resembles an English cottage** (just look at that floral wallpaper) and has long been a favorite spot of the foodies and VIPs who frequent it on the down-low. You must try the hot chocolate served in a saucepan with vanilla whipped cream, as well as the legendary candied chestnut cake, which is sure to enliven your evening.

189 rue de l'Université, Paris 7th.
Hot chocolate €8.

LE DUC

A seafood institution opened more than fifty years ago by foodie mariner Jean Minchelli. Located a stone's throw away from the fashionable Fondation Cartier, we head over to feast on fish, shellfish, and other mouthwatering seafood. Our tip? Go for the very comprehensive Seafood Prix Fixe on offer at lunch, so you can have the experience without breaking your wallet!

243 boulevard Raspail, Paris 14th.
Prix fixe lunch €55.

CAFÉ DE L'ALMA

A short walk from the Eiffel Tower brings you to this neighborhood institution, which recently got a Hamptons-chic facelift. The warm setting offers intimate alcoves, comfortable banquettes, and an elegant terrace where you can relax in an enormous space and extend your evening (almost) indefinitely. We go for trendy cocktails such as the Watermelon Martini before dipping into the brasserie's bestsellers, which all have a modern touch (elbow macaroni with truffles and ham, beef tenderloin au poivre, etc.).

5 avenue Rapp, Paris 7th.
Cocktails from €10.

Café de l'Alma / © Simon Detraz

9 GOURMET
spots to remember

LES PIPELETTES AND ITS DELICIOUS HOUSE-MADE TARTS

31 rue Brézin, Paris 14th

THE JAPANESE-INSPIRED PASTRIES AT MORI YOSHIDA

65 avenue de Breteuil, Paris 7th

THE BISTRO SPECIALITIES AT JAÏS

3 rue Surcouf, Paris 7th

PÈRE & FILS PAR ALLÉNO AND ITS GOURMET BURGER AT BARGAIN PRICES

53-57 rue de Grenelle, Paris 7th

MERSEA AND ITS SEAFOOD STREET FOOD

53-57 Rue de Grenelle, Paris 7th

THE ULTRATENDER MIDDLE EASTERN KEBABS AT SHABESTAN

98 boulevard de Grenelle, Paris 15th

INCREDIBLY DELICATE TWO-MICHELIN-STARRED DISHES BY DAVID TOUTAIN

29 rue Surcouf, Paris 7th

LOVE JUICE BAR, THE MOST REFRESHING SPOT IN THE NEIGHBORHOOD

176 rue de Grenelle, Paris 7th

LE BASILIC AND ITS DREAMY TERRACE

2 rue Casimir-Périer, Paris 7th

2 COFFEE SHOPS FOR A TASTY SNACK BREAK

Ice Creams to Savor

Fruttini © Anne-Charlotte Harnouin

NOIR COFFEE SHOP

With its roastery based in Saint-Ouen and a dozen locations in the capital, Noir is considered the most desirable coffee shop of the moment. Its meticulous decor is ideal for enjoying **an excellent flat white or ultracreamy matcha latte,** along with the must-have cookies and caramel madeleines. And, of course, we never leave without buying the self-serve ground coffee.

9 rue de Luyne, Paris 7ᵗʰ. Cookies €4.50. Flat white €5.

CERTIFIED COFFEE

Head over to open-air foodie destination Beaupassage, home to cutting-edge gourmet spots like **this small, delightful shop** offering delicious caffeinated beverages, including some of the best matcha, chai, and other lattes in the capital. In addition to its terrace, we also come to enjoy its large tables inside, which are ideal for an afternoon coworking session.

83 rue du Bac, Paris 7ᵗʰ. Chai latte €5. Dirty chai €5.50.

GELATERIA GIROTTI

This inviting ice cream shop opened by Terence Hill (yes, the one who starred in all those Westerns!) is all the rage in the 6th. A faithful outpost of his first spot in Umbria, his shop offers some forty superintense flavors (pistachio, hazelnut, coffee, etc.) as well as pastas, salads, and Italian pastries to write home about.

120 boulevard Raspail, Paris 6ᵗʰ. One scoop €3.50.

FRUTTINI

Otherwise known as **the art of making frozen fruit glamorous.** As beautiful and delicious as cake and as light as ice cream, these incredibly refined full-size fruity gems consist of creamy sorbet served in hollowed-out seasonal fruit. The pineapple, date, strawberry, or coconut desserts would make a striking contribution to your next dinner party.

24 rue Saint-Placide, Paris 6ᵗʰ. Pineapple sorbet served in its shell €28.

MARTINE LAMBERT

First opened in Deauville, people are now whispering about its new neighborhood outpost, where you can try **incredible gourmet frozen delights.** Creamy and not overly sweet, we go for the lemon-basil, Mara des Bois strawberry, perfect coffee, or praline, hazelnut, and nougat flavors. Delicious!

39 rue Cler, Paris 7ᵗʰ. One scoop €3.70.

PASSIONATE ABOUT BRUNCH

Vesper / © TheTravelBuds x Vesper

VESPER

This festive restaurant owned by the Fitz Group draws us in with its stunning decor and trendy cocktails, carefully concocted by head bartender Agathe Potel. At night, things get sceney with great DJ sets, but once hangover time arrives, we do the sensible thing and go enjoy its **Japanese-style brunch right on the sunny terrace.** We love the original menu, which allows us to mix it up with morning pastries, a shokupan sandwich, and Japanese-inspired miso pancakes.

*81 avenue Bosquet, Paris 7*th*.*
Brunch menu from €48.

KOZY PARIS

At this spot, which is among the foodiest in the area, **you can share (or not) a decadent brunch with your bestie.** On the menu? Eggs Benedict with either pulled pork, smoked salmon, or halloumi, piles of pancakes served savory or sweet soaked in maple syrup, along with comforting beverages like an iced caramel cortado or a creamy mocha latte.

*79 avenue Bosquet, Paris 7*th*.*
Dishes €12 to €15.

MARCELLE

This restaurant is **the eco-friendly lifestyle** personified. Marcelle doles out a healthy and simple lunch each weekend that features **brunch classics done healthy but 100 percent foodie-approved,** with dishes like tofu "fish" and chips, avocado toast topped with a fried egg, or a chicken club sandwich. For dessert, we love its waffles, available with a variety of spreads and strawberries, or its throwback caramel French toast.

*159 rue de Grenelle, Paris 7*th*. Dishes €12 to €20.*
Pastries from €3.

3

UNIQUE

EXPERIENCES

L'ENTREPÔT

Frédéric Mitterand converted this former printing house into a creative space in the 1970s. It was then taken over by producer Charles Gillibert and gallerist Stéphane Magnon, who now organize amazing programming on its multiple floors, with a focus on arthouse and experimental cinema. There are also an exhibition room and a restaurant where you can sample dishes prepared by the chefs in residence. This **cultural oasis** also offers live jazz concerts every Wednesday!

7 rue Francis de Pressensé, Paris 14th.
Admission to cinema €8.50.

LE CLUB DES POÈTES

This hidden café is the (not so) secret haunt of lovers of literature and sweet nothings. Opened in 1961 by poet Jean-Pierre Rosnay, it is now run by his son, Blaise, who welcome regulars Tuesday through Saturday. The goal? To meet and share a friendly meal "like at home" and, above all, at 9 p.m., **recite poetry together.** Admission is free, provided you know at least one poem by heart! Which one would you choose?

30 rue de Bourgogne, Paris 7th.
Full meal €15 to €25.

YUJ YOGA STUDIO

The first yoga studio in Paris to offer infrared light, which boosts the benefits of doing all the exercises. The room is slightly heated to allow you to completely relax and release all of those toxins. Grab a spot in the dimly lit room (which is covered in candles and twinkling lights) for a Yin Detox or Yoga Flow class, or even a private lesson. We bet you're going to absolutely love it.

11 rue Edmond Valentin, Paris 7th. One class €32.
Ten-class card €275.

Le club des poètes / © Emanuela Cino

Interior Design Stores

Bazaart Nomade / © Camille Delarue

BAZAART NOMADE

This adorable boutique run by the brilliant interior designer Camille Delarue makes you feel right at home. A globe-trotting arts and crafts enthusiast, she brought back from her travels in Africa vases, sculptures, rugs, and other delights made by local creators, who today continue to provide her with sublime items. It's the perfect spot to find some handmade gems or to simply **feel like you're traveling without leaving the capital.**

94 rue du Bac, Paris 7th. Unique pieces €35 to €290. Furniture €500 to €1,600.

LE CUBE ROUGE

This design-focused spot, instantly recognizable with its perfectly red vintage neon sign, is *the* spot to invest in **gorgeous furniture and original pieces** that have made design history. You'll find an astonishing selection of pieces from the 1950s and 1960s, from armchairs to lamps, not to mention tables, all tastefully selected by manager Jérôme Godin. Stunning.

270 boulevard Raspail, Paris 14th. Items €50 to €8,000.

LES AUTRUCHES

A stone's throw away from rue Daguerre, this loftlike Parisian boutique aims to find the rare pearl that will take pride of place in your living room. Opened by two design enthusiast sisters, you'll find **unique designer furniture and lamps.** Could we resist the hand-painted flower plates? The answer is no. And the thick velvet peony couch cover? Not that either.

32 rue Boulard, Paris 14th. Painted plates €75. Sofa cover €190.

LE MARAIS

This is where the *Do It in Paris* editorial staff hides out! The best street food spots, vintage boutiques, stunning art galleries, tearooms— discover the list (it's merely a taste) of our favorite mainstays.

3rd & 4th Arrondissements

Clémence Renoux

OUR FAVORITE EATERIES

GRANDCŒUR

This chic bistro run by Mauro Colagreco, which shares a charming courtyard with the Centre de Danse du Marais, is always a good idea! In particular, to discover its market-driven cuisine, which elevates each ingredient on the plate like a precious gift from nature. The best part is that when the weather is nice, there is a superb terrace away from all the cars.

41 rue du Temple, Paris 4th.
Mains from €25.

SOMA

Celebrities going incognito flock to sit down for a bento box at this Japanese eatery, which is designed like an izakaya. The menu's excellent dishes include shrimp tempura and Agedashi asparagus and eggplant, to be enjoyed with a steaming hot genmaicha (roasted rice) tea.

13 rue de Saintonge, Paris 3rd.
Bento box €20.

LE COLLIER DE LA REINE

It's hard to get ritzier than this sexy brasserie, with its foodie twist on the classic seafood platter. Actors, gallerists, agents, and stylists hurry over to enjoy impeccably sourced shellfish, along with lovely seafood platters that elevate all of the fish, from the most modest to the most refined. Noteworthy: the wine list, which features carefully selected independent producers.

57 rue Charlot, Paris 3rd.
King platter €86.

BONTEMPS

People rush here from all four corners of the capital for its signature sablé cookies. It also has the best lemon cake in Paris. Needless to say, you'll want to book in advance so you can enjoy a magical afternoon at pastry chef Fiona Leluc's tearoom-restaurant, where the sitting room is straight out of a fairy tale, with its shimmering bar, velvet armchairs, vintage opaline light fixtures, and mismatched tableware.

57 rue de Bretagne, Paris 3rd.
Brunch €45.

Bontemps / © Bontemps

KAVIARI DELIKATESSEN

This gourmet delicatessen close to Hôtel de Ville is dedicated to providing carefully sourced fish products. We usually poke our heads in to grab a smoked salmon tartine at lunch, then leave with all of the necessary ingredients for a chic at-home cocktail hour: truffled tarama, blinis, tuna rillettes, dill-marinated herring, and bottarga for grating on top of pasta.

13 rue de l'Arsenal, Paris 4th.

ONII-SAN

When Olivier Léone, cofounder of the Nodaleto shoe brand, teamed up with his pal Arthur Cohen (who's crazy about Japanese culture), it was inevitable that it would result in the sexiest Japanese eatery in the Marais.

All the fashion people flock to this izakaya for its boxes of handrolls, sandos, and sashimi, while eavesdropping on the conversations of the models, creative directors, and stylists at the next table. Excellent touch: the sake menu is explained in detail so you don't get lost.

82 rue des Archives, Paris 3rd.

Onii-San / © Onii-San

ANNE

The best-kept secret of the Marais! Nestled in the romantic courtyard garden of the five-star hotel Le Pavillon de la Reine in the Place des Vosges, the restaurant run by Michelin-starred chef Mathieu Pacaud (L'Ambroisie) is particularly lovely when the weather is nice and you can enjoy a country-chic lunch on the tree-filled terrace. The lowdown: attentive service, elegant dishes, and a dreamy setting. Maybe make a reservation for dinner and stay the night the next time?

28 place des Vosges, Paris 3rd. Prix fixe lunch €49.

Anne / © Anne

LE MARCHÉ DES ENFANTS ROUGES

An absolute must-do in the Marais, visited by passing tourists and neighborhood hipsters alike. Opened in 1615, this is the oldest food market in the capital. In addition to the extraordinary fresh produce, fish, and butcher's stalls, you can find the very best street food from all over the world right here in Paris.

OUR FAVORITES INCLUDE:

COUSCOUS FROM THE MOROCCAN CATERER
(from €9)

BENTO BOXES FROM THE TAEKO JAPANESE STAND
(from €14)

THE 100% ORGANIC OVERSIZE SANDWICHES FROM ALAIN MIAM MIAM
(€13.50)

THE WEST INDIAN BOKITS FROM COROSSOL
(€10)

39 rue de Bretagne, Paris 3rd.
Open Tuesday to Saturday from 8:30 a.m. to 8:30 p.m. and Sundays from 8:30 a.m. to 5 p.m.

10 OBSESSIONS
Our favorite food

THE PASTRIES AT CAFÉ MULOT

6 place des Vosges, Paris 4th

PITAS TO DIE FOR FROM MIZNON

22 rue des Ecouffes, Paris 4th

THE FINGER SANDWICHES AND INSPIRED MACARONS AT CARETTE

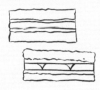

25 place des Vosges, Paris 3rd

THE REFINED BENTO BOXES AT OGATA

16 rue Debelleyme, Paris 3rd

THE AMERICAN CANDIES AT SWEET ESCAPE

19 rue des Ecouffes, Paris 4th

SMALL STUFFED VEGETABLES PROVENCAL AT CHEZ JANOU
2 rue Roger Verlomme, Paris 3rd

THE EXCELLENT CORSICAN DISHES AT L'ALIVI

27 rue du Roi de Sicile, Paris 4th

FOODPORN SANDWICHES AT ALAIN MIAM MIAM

26 rue Charlot, Paris 3rd

THE PRINCESS CAKE AT FIKA
11 rue Payenne, Paris 3rd

THE PÂTÉ-EN-CROÛTE AT MAISON VÉROT
38 rue de Bretagne, Paris 3rd

MY FAVORITES

Do IT IN
PARIS

MY FAVORITES

3 GALLERIES
THAT WILL NEVER DISAPPOINT YOU

Since they're located just five minutes apart from one another, we take the opportunity to go for a stroll in the Marais and visit hip, cutting-edge art galleries like **Thaddaeus Ropac** (*7 rue Debelleyme*), **Perrotin** (*76 rue de Turenne*), and **Galerie Karsten Greve** (*5 rue Debelleyme*), three major names in the contemporary art world that each present the most interesting artists of the moment in extraordinary spaces (and with free admission). Regardless of what's on, great surprises always await.

Galerie Perrotin / © Emanuele Cino

Maison Suisen / © Maxime Frogé

A SPA TO TRY

ONCE IN YOUR LIFE

Have you heard of a *ryokan*? This traditional Japanese inn is distinguished by the handcrafted materials that comprise it: straw ceiling, bamboo floor, and washi paper walls. Proud heir to this truly Japanese practice, **Maison Suisen** strives to take care of the whole body so that it works better, all in a soothing setting. There are green teas, meditation, and massage—especially shiatsu. We feel great, completely cut off from the frenzy of the world and its stresses— it's one way to recharge your batteries between twelve and two.

7 rue de Thorigny, Paris 3ʳᵈ.
Massage €140.

THE BEST
VINTAGE
STORES IN THE MARAIS

LAPIN BOUTIQUE
THE MOST 1970s

It's impossible not to swoon over **the boldly colored 1970s gems** that Florencia, who's obsessed with Courrèges trenches and print dresses, has managed to amass. We absolutely love that Lapin Boutique's winding clothes racks hold nothing but carefully curated favorites, both designer and not, grouped by type of clothing and color. No wonder rummaging here is truly a pleasure.
9 rue Oberkampf, Paris 11th.
White woolen skirt suit €130.

VINTAGE PARIS
THE MOST LUXURIOUS

Frequented by actresses, stylists, singers, and fashionistas, this spot is the most popular vintage shop of the Paris smart set. Let's be clear: it's *the* must-go boutique when you're a devoted fan of luxury vintage. There are bags, watches, and sunglasses. **Hermès, Chanel, and**

Gucci gems make our knees go weak.
97 rue Vieille du Temple, Paris 3rd.
Chanel shopping tote €2,000.

TWICE PARIS
THE MOST ACCESSIBLE

This place embodies the young guard of female entrepreneurs riding the wave of vintage obsession and good deals. After graduating from business school, Elena Le Fur launched Twice Paris, a roving, temporary secondhand store in the Marais—be sure to follow the locations on Instagram, where she sells never-worn (or almost new) brand-name pieces previously offered to influencers, including Sézane knits, Rouje dresses, and Polène bags.
128 rue de Turenne, Paris 3rd.
Claudie Pierlot dress €110.

PLAISIR PALACE
THE MOST CUTTING-EDGE

A leading figure in contemporary art and an important fashion

collector, Didier Barroso has dreamed up this "neo-pop Eden," which brings together various outrageous pieces. A true enthusiast, the clothing collector offers up finds from the 1970s to 2000 by **Courrèges, Alaïa, Yves Saint Laurent, Céline, Lanvin, and Vivienne Westwood,** which the stylists of *Emily in Paris* find particularly thrilling.
3 rue Paul Dubois, Paris 3rd.
Yves Saint Laurent dress €600.

EN VOITURE SIMONE
THE COOLEST

The models who flock here each fashion week to get dressed up for the neighboring showrooms have made it their shopping headquarters. This little boutique offers strong, wearable pieces, not hesitating to combine items—like collectible Mickey Mouse T-shirts with fringed jackets and denim pieces. It's **Isabel Marant mixed with the ranch spirit of Ralph Lauren.**
6 rue du Perche, Paris 3rd.
Coveralls €140.

Window-Shopping

Merci © Merci

MERCI

It's hard to spend less than a full hour at Merci—**the concept store in the Haut Marais** is brimming with treasures for men and women alike: Isabel Marant blouses, Birkenstock sandals, Justine Clenquet jewelry, Carhartt caps, as well as pieces from emerging designers. On the home decor front, there's a substantial selection with gorgeous tableware, bedding, lamps, vases, and curtains. Note: there's an amazing garden-level eatery where, come lunchtime, you can sink your teeth into a tartine.
*111 boulevard Beaumarchais, Paris 3*rd*.*
Canvas shopping tote €95.

MIISTA

While Miista shoes may have conquered the world, showing up on the feet of "It" girls like Bella Hadid and Kendall Jenner, the little boutique on rue Turenne remains a secret. Designer Laura Villasenin's style MO? **Nineties-style pairs** including ankle boots, loafers, clogs, and boots that give you that edgy London look, in patent leather, denim, or cowhide, with signature square tips—there is even a fabulous ready-to-wear collection.
*31 rue Charlot, Paris 3*rd*. Pairs from €175.*

TOM GREYHOUND

It's difficult to remain reasonable in this boutique that brings together the most bankable brands of the moment for men and women (**Jacquemus, JW Anderson, Coperni, etc.**) as well as the new guard of designers. What do they have in common? Elegant minimalism. Jackets, shirts, dresses, hats, knitwear, sneakers, and jewelry are available on perfectly arranged racks, ready to be tried on. Self-restraint required!
*19 rue de Saintonge, Paris 3*rd*.*
Courrèges cap €160.

PAN

This is **heaven for lovers of vintage decor who can't be bothered to bargain hunt.** Milena and her husband, Guillaume, have done the work for us at this bric-a-brac store with friendly prices, where we want to buy everything—vases, plates, jars, candlesticks, all carefully curated. Also first-rate: a selection of new, ultrafunky objects, such as a banana vase, a fox carafe, and other Lucky Cats items—great for sprucing up your living room with unusual pieces sure to impress.

56 rue de Turbigo, Paris 3rd.
Opaline vase €19.50.

EN SELLE MARCEL

Close to the rue de Rivoli cycle path, bike addicts from all over get together in this beautiful shop where experienced professionals are responsible for finding the bicycle that suits you best, **from a classic Electra to the latest electric Schindelhauer.** And for those who are still undecided, there's also an excellent long-term rental option, which includes insurance against theft as well as a fast and complete maintenance service.

22 rue de la Perle, Paris 3rd.
Electric bikes from €2,199.

Pan / © Pan

Secret Gardens

Square Saint-Gilles GrandVeneur © Eugenia Gula

SQUARE SAINT-GILLES GRAND VENEUR

The seventeenth-century mansion encircling this square changed hands many times before being divided into apartments. Luckily, you can take advantage of its **dreamy garden smack-dab in the center of the Marais,** complete with climbing roses, stone benches, and soft grass. Since it's not visible from the street, you'll need to cross a discreet portico. Grab a good book and a sandwich before you do.

Entrance at 9 rue du Grand Veneur, Paris 3ʳᵈ.

Jardin des Rosiers / © Emanuela Cino

JARDIN DES ROSIERS – JOSEPH-MIGNERET

You just need to know the trick! Accessible only by a small, covered passageway, this nearly 23,000-sq.-ft paradise is the result of **combining three gardens belonging to private mansions** from the seventeenth century. The obligatory move? Sit down next to the large fig or orange trees, which are deliciously fragrant.

Entrance at 10 rue des Rosiers, Paris 4th.

MONTMARTRE & PIGALLE

Strolls to conquer the highest point in Paris,
romantic dinners for two, and evenings in
the great outdoors. More romantic than ever,
Montmartre continues to inspire us!

9th & 18th Arrondissements

Clémence Renoux

OUR FAVORITE EATERIES

LE BON LA BUTTE

While we love the village spirit that prevails in Montmartre, we also adore the unique vibe of its restaurants. Starting with the neo-bistro of David Polin, a self-taught chef and friendly host (gotta stay to true to those Marseillais roots!) who turns out **clever, comforting dishes,** including an Angus hanger steak with mashed potatoes that we can't help but order every time we come! Also first-rate: the super wine selection. Enjoy the ride!

102 ter rue Lepic, Paris 18ᵗʰ. House-made terrine €11.

L'OUZERI

After the success of Etsi, mere steps away, **the latest Mediterranean taverna from French and Greek chef Mikaela Liaroutsos** (formerly of Lignac, Rostang) summons up her greatest childhood memories from Athens, with a street food twist. We often share an octopus salad, grilled pitas Meridas, and oregano fries, toasting to future vacations with glasses of Greek wine or ouzo, that typical anise-flavored aperitif. All that's missing is the sea.

41 rue du Ruisseau, Paris 18ᵗʰ. Meridas €14.

CAFÉ DE LUCE

We still adore the cooking of Amandine Chaignot (Pouliche), now established in Montmartre, all the better to jibe with the neighborhood's hearty instincts. The result includes beef cheek shepherd's pie, spring chicken with morels to be shared, and excellent **knife-cut tartare with a generous showering of caviar.** Tip: save room for dessert—there are crème brulée and chocolate lava cake.

2 rue des Trois Frères, Paris 18ᵗʰ. Tartare with caviar €38.

Le Bon La Butte / © Emanuela Cino

Café de Luce / © Emanuela Cino

BARBOT

Clinking glasses around lovely plates of seafood is the common theme of Les Maquereaux spots, which have truly become summer rendezvous points along the Seine. In Pigalle, we go from a dance hall feel to **a bohemian betting-on-the-races mood, where a chill vibe and good humor reign.** Whole fish, whelks mayonnaise, parsleyed razor clams, and moules frites are served at lunch and dinner in a friendly setting, with a large terrace for when the weather's nice.
47-49 avenue Trudaine, Paris 9th. Whelks €10.

SALE E PEPE

Montmartre residents would prefer that we not divulge the name of this Italian trattoria, which serves **one of the best wood-fired pizzas in Paris.** Our favorites include the effective Marinara (tomato sauce, garlic, parsley), the signature Della Casa (tomato sauce, mozzarella, spicy salami, egg, pepper, and olives), and the Bomba Calabrese with pecorino shavings. We share slices underneath the fun Arcimboldo repro, and promise we'll come back to try the lasagna alla siciliana; it's the bomb, baby.
30 rue Ramey, Paris 18th. Pizza Regina €13.50, lasagna €14.

RIV'K

This sunny yellow storefront is the stronghold of Rebecca Rohmer, who learned from the greats (Christian Constant, Yannick Alléno, Dominique Bouchet) and turns out **delicious Israeli dishes.** It's easy at Riv'k, because we love everything: the ultracolorful decor peppered with vintage items, bold shaken cocktails, and fusion cooking that marries Israeli flavors (schnitzels, pitas, latkes, etc.) with Asian spices. Follow the path to happiness!
35 rue Véron, Paris 18th. Pita with shredded beef, cheese, and tahini €28.

HECTAR

Rare are the dishes that make you feel like you know the chef the second you pick up a fork! His name is Benjamin Schmitt and he turns out snappy dishes at his South Pigalle restaurant, where you'll discover **surprise seasonings and condiments with every bite** of dishes like crispy sweetbreads, gnocchi with asparagus, and strawberry rhubarb pavlova. The menu changes depending on what comes in and on the whims of the chef, who always finds the perfect wines to pair with the food. Not surprisingly, that's the chef's other hobby, and his other half's profession.
41 rue Catherine de La Rochefoucauld, Paris 9th. Prix fixe lunch €26.

ODETTE MA FILLE !

Have you ever had a *coca*? The little savory turnovers, a pied noir version of Spanish empanadas, are served at this tiny yet bold eatery where you'll feel right at home. Inspired by her grandmother Odette's favorite recipe, Judith now holds the secret and regales us with her handheld cocas stuffed with shakshuka, peas, or caramelized onions. The fantastic sweet version with chocolate, ricotta, and lemon is truly a find!
16 rue de Trétaigne, Paris 18th. Daily prix fixe menu €11.

Hectar / © Victor Bellot

THAT PARTY LIFE!

Start with one and continue to the other: our two sure shots for a lively evening.

DOUBLEVIE

All the cool kids in the north of Paris are convening at Doublevie, which, in just a few months, has become **the rendezvous point for tables of friends come to feast,** toast, and dance. Yes, dancing, since the electrifying sounds of vinyl records get the crowds grooving on the lower mezzanine. Yet it's upstairs and on the level above (by the gigantic *table d'hôtes*) where the excellent Mediterranean share plates and bottles of natural wine keep us extending our evenings at this incredible 1940s building with large glass windows.

2 rue Poulet, Paris 18th. Bottle of wine from €29.

MIKADO DANCING

Access the Mikado, hidden in the basement of the Hôtel Rochechouart, through the door on the left in the lobby. A former gambling den and a veritable institution of the Parisian night in the 1960s and 1980s, the club has gotten a stylish facelift with a Japanese influence. Wooden panels and lanterns punctuate an art deco interior that harkens back to the 1920s, when you'd slouch on lovely golden velvet couches between flirting sessions. **The electrifying DJ sets and always excellent cocktails** keep us coming back.

55 boulevard de Rochechouart, Paris 9th. Mikado cocktail €14.

Mikado dancing / © Ludovic Balay

WE'D CROSS PARIS FOR . . .

BOULOM

With Julien Duboué, you should never trust appearances. His latest prank? Stashing the trendiest eatery in Paris inside the backroom of an elegant, retro-style neighborhood bakery. You have no choice but to pass the pastry counter and wall of breads to get to the main room, which is checkered with large tables under a green ceiling. The highlight of the show? **Every weekend, there's an enormous brunch** with seafood galore, terrines, eggs mimosa, hot mains, and, of course, a very large selection of breads and breakfast pastries.

181 rue Ordener, Paris 18th.
Brunch €49.

3 HOTEL
STAYS
TO BOOK NOW

A BRUNCH AT MONSIEUR ARISTIDE

This perfectly cozy boutique hotel offers **a voyage through the bohemian spirit of Montmartre** and the Belle Époque. From the moment you pass the counter in the lobby, a space-time loop is created, revealing a jukebox, velvet couches, a terrazzo floor, a mahogany bar, bamboo armchairs, domed ceiling lights, ceramic lamps, old radios in the rooms, and stair runners. On Sundays, you can sit down to enjoy a very hearty brunch in the charming setting.

3 rue Aristide Bruant, Paris 18th. Brunch €36.

A DRINK AT LE TRÈS PARTICULIER

Brad Pitt and Johnny Depp are just a few of the people who've stayed at this pocket-size hotel tucked away at the end of a tree-lined alley. **A former residence of the Hermès family,** the Hôtel Particulier Montmartre offers five suites, and, most notably, an idyllic country garden reminiscent of an impressionist painting. You don't need to stay at the hotel to reap the benefits: the on-site restaurant and bar have everything you need for a very romantic evening. The Très Particulier's red armchairs and signature cocktails will get you in the right mood.

23 avenue Junot Pavillon D, Paris 18th. Cocktails from €15.

Monsieur Aristide / © CDSE

DINNER WITH A VIEW AT THE TERRASS' HOTEL

Parisians have made this hilltop hotel in the heart of Montmartre an essential meeting spot, for its yoga classes and treatments at the Nuxe spa, but, above all, for its **incredible** **rooftop with a view of all of Paris** (including the Eiffel Tower). If it's too cold to have a drink on the terrace, reserve a table and gaze at the sky from the panoramic restaurant, Edmond. It's perched on the seventh floor and offers fusion cuisine from chef Santiago Guerrero.

12–14 rue Joseph de Maistre, Paris 18th. Signature cocktail €17.

Do IT IN
PARIS

MY FAVORITES

MY FAVORITES

Woods gallery / © Woods gallery

Barkers & Brothers / © Barkers & Brothers

THE CONCEPT STORE TO TRUST
THE WOODS GALLERY

Opened five years ago by Laurent and Simon, and five minutes from the Sacré-Cœur, this home decor boutique offers a selection of highly desirable products to **lend a touch of fun to your decor.** Our favorites include: the cult-favorite Ultrafragola mirror designed by Ettore Sottsass, Aykasa pastel storage bins, a gift set of orange-flavored toothpaste, a Playboy poster, and a ceramic fish-shaped carafe, not to mention a cutting-edge selection of books and magazines, along with designer furniture.

*22 rue André del Sarte, Paris 18*th*. Fish carafe €64.*

A MEETING PLACE FOR COOL DOGS
BARKERS & BROTHERS

This concept store for canines is one-stop shopping for the most stylish essentials. It belongs to Marie Dardaine, a former advertising executive and overprotective mother to her Akita. The shop has an assortment of colorful accessories (think Carhartt, Maxbone, Monsieur Hardi, etc.), a well-equipped grooming center upstairs, and even a little coffee shop. Don't leave without offering your pooch a delicious puppuccino, the ultimate treat, made with coconut milk.

*8 rue Androuet, Paris 18*th*. Dog bath €25 per hour.*

Musée de la vie romantique / © Emanuela Cino

Jardins Renoir / © Jardins Renoir

MUSÉE DE LA VIE ROMANTIQUE

We dream of moving in. While we adore visiting this cult museum for its fascinating exhibitions, we also love taking a break in the tearoom. Rose Bakery turns out the best carrot cake in Paris, along with scones, sandwiches, quiches, brownies, and all kinds of hot beverages. You can enjoy the treats under the greenhouse with its winter garden vibe or out on the picturesque terrace.

16 rue Chaptal, Paris 9th.
Carrot cake €6.50.

JARDINS RENOIR

This is the best-kept secret of La Butte. Behind the door of the Musée de Montmartre lies a sublime garden inspired by Renoir's masterpiece *Le Bal du Moulin de la Galette*. The artist opened his studio here in 1876 (jealous). We go after visiting the current (always interesting) exhibition or get a garden-only ticket to admire the view of the vines and northern Paris. Then we settle in for **an afternoon tea worthy of Downton Abbey,** taken in direct view of the well-manicured lawns.

12 rue Cortot, Paris 18th.
Garden-only ticket €5.

Secret Gardens

Playground Duperré / © Emanuela Cino

MUST-SEES AND DOS

HAVE A LAUGH IN THE COMPANY OF DRAG QUEENS AT MADAME ARTHUR CABARET
75 bis rue des Martyrs, Paris 18th

TOUCH THE DALIDA BUST BY SCULPTOR ASLAN FOR GOOD LUCK
rue de l'Abreuvoir, Paris 18th

FIND THE FABRIC FOR YOUR NEXT SET OF CURTAINS AT THE MARCHÉ SAINT-PIERRE
2 rue Charles Nodier, Paris 18th

TAKE PART IN THE HARVEST FESTIVAL

ENJOY A 100% TOURISTY EVENING AT THE MOULIN ROUGE
82 boulevard de Clichy, Paris 18th

OR IF YOU PREFER, DANCE ALL NIGHT
98 boulevard de Clichy, Paris 18th

PLAY PÉTANQUE AT THE SQUARE SUZANNE BUISSON
7 bis rue Girardon, Paris 18th

FIND THE TOMBS OF ÉMILE ZOLA AND MICHEL BERGER AT THE MONTMARTRE CEMETERY
20 avenue Rachel, Paris 18th

WATCH A BASKETBALL GAME AT THE PLAYGROUND DUPERRÉ
22 rue Duperré, Paris 9th

Montorgueil, Sentier & Les Halles

From Sentier to Les Halles, and passing through Montorgueil and Étienne Marcel, the streets might intersect, but they're all very different! Each one has its own vibe, its old reliables, and its new hot spots. The former Belly of Paris has great restaurants and is asserting its foodie status with iconic destinations, some of which have been around for several centuries.

1st, 2nd & 3rd Arrondissements

Sandra Serpero

OUR FAVORITE EATERIES

SHABOUR

This unexpected Michelin-starred bar is the most popular Parisian stronghold of Israeli star chef Assaf Granit and his partners in crime: Dan Yosha, Uri Navon, and Tomer Lanzman (Balagan, Tekés). In its exposed stone interior, Shabour proudly leans into its rough side, assembling guests around an open kitchen studded with candles. We sit elbow to elbow, lulled by the opera soundtrack, which provides the necessary dose of drama to the irresistibly generous cooking.

19 rue Saint Sauveur, Paris 2nd.
Prix fixe lunch €76.

BAMBOU

All the Parisian hipsters rush to Bambou, blown over by the unusual 5,382-sq.-ft. space, which nostalgically evokes the grand bars of Asia. There are small and large sitting areas, a remarkable smoking room, **a heavenly terrace, and a sexy cocktail bar** where a DJ sets the mood. The menu features glamorous and delicate Thai cuisine: pad thai with shrimp, caramel chicken wrapped in pandan leaf, crispy calamari, and sea bream tartare.

23 rue des Jeûneurs, Paris 2nd.
Spicy green curry chicken €26.

CAFÉ COMPAGNON

Open continuously from breakfast to dinner, this spot, which captures the taste of the times, checks all the boxes for lovely and delicious cuisine. Chef Alexandre Rotaru's gourmet bistro features **travel-inspired cuisine in a stylish setting.** The cherry on

top: a serene jewel of a terrace where you can linger.

22-26 rue Léopold Bellan, Paris 2nd.
Gnocchi with sage €25.

À L'ÉPI D'OR

Partnering with his wife, Élodie, **chef Jean-François Piège is at the helm of the kitchen** in this charming restaurant dating back to the 1920s, located just a few steps (in stilettos) from the Louboutin boutique. Nothing (or almost nothing) has changed in the decor, which remains full of ambiance. Go with the flow of the Michelin-starred chef's stylish weekly specials, or opt for the bistro menu's mainstays: lamb so soft it's served with a spoon, pâté en croûte, steak tartare with fries, croque madame, and rice pudding.

25 rue Jean-Jacques Rousseau, Paris 1st.
Chopped steak and fries €27.

À l'Epi d'or © Bernadette Chiala

Granite / © Granite

LES AMIS DE MESSINA

A defender of good, healthy cooking, chef Ignazio Messina offers his clients a direct flight to his native land. The menu explores **the typical flavors of Sicily** with charming, simply delicious dishes. The must-try? The crazy good zucchini cake with vanilla and mascarpone cream—it will make you want to keep coming back.

81 rue Réaumur, Paris 2nd. Torta Mamma Lina €8.

CHEZ GEORGES

This genuine, timeless bistro (truly—it's been there since 1864) located right next to the Place des Victoires is frequented by Parisian high-society types and film celebrities. Chez Georges offers a nice slice of nostalgia in its charming dining room, which features moleskin banquettes, a handwritten menu, and its resolutely old-school cooking.

1 rue du Mail, Paris 2nd. Sweetbreads with morels €49.

GRANITE

This **successful restaurant, which has one Michelin star,** is the stronghold of young chef and *Meilleur Ouvrier de France* Tom Meyer. We love to savor the chef's striking combinations of ingredients, all delicately prepared and served in a low-key setting. Ultramodern with lots of heart, Granite's cooking favors Île-de-France products, vegetables, and a zero-waste philosophy. Dishes pair well with one of the nearly five hundred wines in its cellar, which features important players from the new wine-growing scene.

6 rue Bailleul, Paris 1st. Prix fixe lunch €75.

THREE QUINTESSENTIAL BRASSERIES

Aux Crus de Bourgogne / © Emanuela Cino

AUX CRUS DE BOURGOGNE

This legendary restaurant (open since 1902), which André Malraux used to frequent, has regained all its luster under the leadership of the Dumant family. The period decor has a ravishing charm, with white tablecloths, **elegant service, and homemade "all-butter" bistro cooking.** The lineup of great bistro classics includes leeks mimosa, tagliatelle with morels, and beef tenderloin with sauce au poivre.

3 rue Bachaumont, Paris 2nd.
Mains from €25. Beef bourguignon €29.

L'ESCARGOT MONTORGUEIL

This sublime spot, opened in 1832, is awash in Second Empire details, and is even classified as a historic monument. The restaurant gives pride of place to its legendary recipe for escargots de Bourgogne, which has been passed down from generation to generation, perpetuating a cult expertise that puts high-quality products and an intensely parsleyed house-made butter to excellent use. The menu also contains those **classics of French gastronomy** that we unabashedly enjoy: frogs' legs, vol-au-vent, sweetbreads, and crêpes Suzette.

38 rue Montorgueil, Paris 1st.
Six escargots €12.

LE PETIT BOUILLON PHARAMOND

On a sunny and joyfully animated little square of Les Halles, this traditionally Norman bouillon, with its extraordinary Belle Époque decor, offers homemade bistro fare, delighting with **comforting dishes at very low prices:** eggs mimosa, Caen-style tripe, braised ham with mashed potatoes, baked elbow macaroni with truffled cream, and tarte tatin. Even better: you can rent out one of the low-lit sitting rooms to host an unforgettable birthday feast.

24 rue de la Grande Truanderie, Paris 1st.
Share plates from €7.50.

Le Petit Bouillon Pharamond / © Le Petit Bouillon Pharamond

Comfort Food

Junk / © Junk

ECHO

A little slice of California right in Sentier, with a sigh-inducing menu that allows for some excellent indulgent forays. On the menu: devilishly clever sandwiches like the Morning Sandy, which features a smash burger, cheddar cheese, and a fried egg, or the grilled cheese with gouda-raclette.
95 rue d'Aboukir, Paris 2nd.
Sandwiches from €12.

BONESHAKER DONUTS

Pastry fairy Amanda Bankert, who grew up in the United States, no doubt makes **the best doughnuts in Paris!** They're prepared in-house with organic ingredients, from the dough to the garnishes, right down to the icing. Our fave? The Fluffernutter: peanut butter, marshmallow icing, and slivers of praline. A real knockout!
86 rue d'Aboukir, Paris 2nd. Doughnuts from €3.70.

JUNK

This burger bar offers smash burgers you should try (at least) once in your life. The unique recipe consists of a brioche bun, perfectly cooked beef patty, extramelty American cheese, and an impeccably spiced secret sauce. Choose from sizes S to XXL depending on your hunger.
114 rue Montmartre, Paris 2nd.
Burgers €5.90 to €16.90.

CALI SISTERS

A must-go for any foodie hipster in the capital, especially on the weekend, when they offer a house brunch—a truly foodporn-worthy amalgamation of the best of the West Coast. There are savory and sweet pancakes topped with maple butter, a perfect egg sandwich with spicy cheddar sauce, and even an addictive brioche French toast topped with whipped cream.
17 rue Notre Dame des Victoires, Paris 2nd. Brunch €30.

BARS WITH
OUTDOOR
SPACES WE LOVE

AU ROCHER DE CANCALE
The quintessential spot to see and be seen!
78 rue Montorgueil, Paris 2nd

THE HOXTON PARIS
The epicenter of Parisian cool, with a cobblestoned court that's perfect for enjoying an aperitif with a group of friends.
30–32 rue du Sentier, Paris 2nd

Le Compas / © Emanuela Cino

LE COMPAS
The biggest terrace on the street, vibrant and always packed.
62 rue Montorgueil, Paris 2nd

HÔTEL DU SENTIER
A terrace that's like a little village square, tree-lined and sunny, where you can bliss out over a great breakfast from 7 a.m. onward.
48 rue du Caire, Paris 2nd

HÔTEL MADAME RÊVE
Enjoy a glass of champagne or a cocktail with your significant other on this ridiculously cool rooftop, which offers a mesmerizing view.
48 rue du Louvre, Paris 1st

L'EMPIRE BRASSERIE
The best Sunday morning option if you're looking to enjoy coffee under the sun.
108 rue Réaumur, Paris 2nd

Hoxton Paris / © The Hoxton Paris

SWEET PLEASURES

STOHRER

The oldest pastry shop in Paris, and a true piece of heritage (its walls have historic monument status!), was founded in 1730 by Nicolas Stohrer, pastry chef to King Louis XV and the inventor of the rum baba. We also hustle over for its lovely puits d'amour, magnificent religieuse à l'ancienne, out of this world crispy caramel gateau Saint-Honoré, and intensely flavored éclairs.

51 rue Montorgueil, Paris 2nd.
Rum baba €5.60.

Stohrer / © Alexandre Guirkinger

BOULANGERI

TERROIRS D'AVENIR

AGRICULTURE PAYSANNE
DEPUIS 2008

—

DU MARDI
AU DIMANCHE MATIN

RUE DU NIL:
A FOODIE HAUNT

Under chef Grégory Marchand's leadership, the once sketchy, now charming rue du Nil, nestled a stone's throw from rue Réaumur, has turned into a food kingdom whose reputation has extended way beyond Paris's borders. A veritable 2nd arrondissement icon, this hot spot is frequented by all the neighborhoods' residents, who come to do their shopping, along with foodies from here and abroad heading to Frenchie and its outposts.

Terroirs d'Avenir / © Emanuela Cino

FROM STREET NUMBERS ONE TO TEN, YOU CAN FIND:

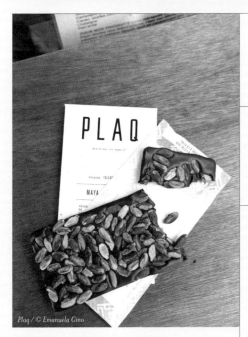

Plaq / © Emanuela Cino

PLAQ

And its exquisite chocolates whose
scent fills the entire street.

From €4

FRENCHIE CAVISTE

With more than 350 wines on offer.

*Bottles €7 to €550
for a Batard Montrachet grand cru*

TERROIRS D'AVENIR

You can fill your basket with top-quality
products from the fruit and vegetable
market, butcher shop, fish shop, and
excellent bakery.

Mixed white and whole grain bread from €3.50

L'ARBRE À CAFÉ

With its grand cru coffee, sold as whole
beans or ground.

From €12.90

FRENCHIE BAR À VINS

A relaxed spot to share some food and
have a drink.

*Wines by the glass from €6
Share plates from €8*

FRENCHIE

Michelin-starred restaurant where Greg
Marchand offers a chef's tasting menu
at dinner.

€140

Frenchie / © Emanuela Cino

GET IMMERSED IN CULTURE

FORUM DES IMAGES

All the richness of the seventh art is here. **Celebrating the expansive range of film,** the Forum des Images offers an eclectic program with more than two thousand screenings per year, a dozen yearly festivals, and many thematic events open to the public. Last but not least is its incredible collection of more than eight thousand films, which you can watch for free.
2 rue du Cinéma, Forum des Halles, Paris 1st. Admission €7.20.

Bourse de commerce / © Emanuela Cino

BOURSE DE COMMERCE

Contemporary art has found its greatest hideout, under the dome of this beautiful historic monument. François Pinault (a businessman who needs no introduction) made his Parisian dream a reality, installing works from his own collections and those of his favorite artists in this structure located at the edge of the Jardin des Halles and just a five minute walk from the Louvre. This is where heritage meets contemporary design.
2 rue de Viarmes, Paris 1st. Admission €14.

LA GAÎTÉ LYRIQUE

After closing and changing direction, La Gaîté Lyrique has affirmed its new position as **an everyday spot dedicated to artistic creation and social engagement.** On the program: workshops and conferences, as well as concerts and exhibitions. Its growing food offerings highlight the Bandes de Cheffes collective, a charitable, eco-friendly catering service that helps refugee women join the working world. Tip from our editors: go for the weekend brunch in the historic hall, which features a generous gourmet prix fixe buffet.
3 bis rue Papin, Paris 3rd. Brunch €28.

LIBRAIRIE PETITE ÉGYPTE

Here's the only general-interest bookstore in the neighborhood—and it's invaluable! It's impossible to miss—you can't help but see its green storefront. Friendly Alexis Argyroglo, master of the house, is never stingy with his recommendations, and caters to a broad audience, offering **a ton of literary titles** and even children's and comic book sections. Note: there's always something going on, between the many types of conferences, seminars, and discussions.
35 rue des Petits Carreaux, Paris 2nd.

Where to Shop Vintage

SOLDES

weDoSTUDIOS

Bobby /© Emanuela Cino

KILIWATCH

The concept store. Open since 1996, it mixes the **best vintage discoveries** from around the world with new clothing, accessories, and designer jewelry, in a 6,458-sq.-ft. space.
64 rue Tiquetonne, Paris 2ⁿᵈ.
Dickies overalls €89.

EPISODE

Direct from the Netherlands, this well-curated thrift store with reasonable prices is brimming with timeless fashion pieces, especially from its favorite eras—the 1970s, 1980s, and 1990s.
12-16 rue Tiquetonne, Paris 2ⁿᵈ. Levi's 501 jeans €40.

BOBBY

This **cool boutique-secondhand store** is a fashion temple where you can find clothing from luxury houses or trendy designers: Koché, Balenciaga, Escada, and more.
89 rue Réaumur, Paris 2ⁿᵈ.
Christian Lacroix mesh T-shirt €75.

Palais-Royal & Vendôme

The Louvre, rue Saint-Honoré, the
Tuileries—it's hard to get more touristy than
the capital's nerve center. All the treasures of
French heritage are here. But true Parisians
know that from Palais-Royal to Vendôme,
you can also sit down to eat in the most
beautiful tearooms and the most incredible,
of-the-moment restaurants (and all in
between two cultural visits that
will take your breath away).

1st & 2nd Arrondissements

Clémence Renoux

SNACK TIME

SÉBASTIEN GAUDARD

The meet-up place for the nouveau chic set is this gourmet tea salon (with a très Vendôme vibe) that Sébastien Gaudard, the gifted pastry chef from rue des Martyrs, opened opposite the Tuileries. His MO? The art of reconnecting with the old-school French tea salon tradition. The sweets, which are as delicate as they are nostalgic, include our sugar obsession: a caramelized cream puff made from choux pastry, filled with lightly whipped cream and topped with crunchy caramel. The Paris-Brest, another must, was a unanimous hit!
3 rue des Pyramides, Paris 1st. Caramelized cream puff €8.20.

Sébastien Gaudard / © Sébastien Gaudard

MAISON VERLET

Hidden upstairs at this space straight out of Downton Abbey is a **supercozy tearoom,** perfect for having a chat in peace and quiet, away from indiscreet ears. Here the signature beverage is a grand cru coffee, artisanally roasted nearby in the café's own roastery in Palais-Royal. Go ahead and do justice to your classic iced latte, tucking into such guilty pleasures as house-made waffles with whipped cream and chocolate sauce, a caramel fontainebleau, or a red berry pavlova—yummy!
256 rue Saint-Honoré, Paris 1st. Viennese coffee €6.50.

CAFÉ KITSUNÉ

This small coffee shop owned by the brand with the fox on it is a must-do. Located under the arcade of the Montpensier gallery, it offers a direct view of the Palais-Royal gardens. You might need to wait in the (at times long) line, but then you'll be able to discreetly observe the incognito celebrities in their Ray-Bans as they await their specialty coffee, flat white, or chai latte. We personally also order a piece of the carrot cake, unless we have just spent our lunch hour devouring one of its devilishly good chicken katsu and mayo sandos.
51 galerie de Montpensier, Paris 1st. Matcha latte €6.

ANGELINA

It's **the most iconic tea salon in Paris,** built in 1903 and a fixture of rue de Rivoli, not to mention Gabrielle Chanel's chosen place to rendezvous. The legend is so enduring and the art nouveau decor so spectacular that you should definitely play the tourist game at least once in your life . . . and why not even more? If there are no reservations available, we slip in at teatime to try the house classics: a perfect club sandwich, a chestnut Mont Blanc (the signature pastry), a napoleon or éclair, and, of course, the hot chocolate and whipped cream, which requires no introduction.
226 rue de Rivoli, Paris 1st.
Afternoon tea €25. Hot chocolate €8.90.

Angelina / © Angelina

Our Favorite Eateries

Nhome / © Pierre Lucet-Penato

NHOME

Foodies who think they've seen it all, take note. And spoiler alert—this is a cool combination: a unique surprise menu, **a beautiful, vaulted cellar, and ultrachill service.** You've hit the jackpot! Indeed chef Matan Zaken has always fantasized about a fine-dining restaurant where all the cooks would bring out a surprise dish to the dining room, assembling a menu that changes depending on what comes in—smoked eel, foie gras, onion and turnip broth, asparagus with seaweed and wild garlic, blue lobster with artichokes—right down to the signature dessert: an incredible bowl of roasted and puffed grains. Now when are we going back?

41 rue de Montpensier, Paris 1st.
Prix fixe tasting menu €115, wine pairing €65.

ALFRED

This chic brasserie, tucked along the street where Alfred de Musset once lived, checks all the boxes: **a Mondrian-style decor and gourmet modern bistro cuisine** dreamed up by Alexia Duchêne. The chef breathes new life into the great classics of traditional bistro cuisine and ensures a wonderful evening from the moment you enter, with eggs mimosa sprinkled with chives or spunky seasonal vegetable tarte tatin, followed by a juicy beef tenderloin topped with a whisky au poivre sauce. As far as dessert goes, don't let the delicate Dunes Blanches with chocolate sauce get away.

8 rue du Mont-Thabor, Paris 1st.
Beef Wellington €33.

Mer & Coquillage / © Ilya Kagan

MER & COQUILLAGE

Favorite alert! In this wood-paneled interior reminiscent of a luxury liner, chef Mathieu Poirier, who's obsessed with excellent fish, sets to work taking seafood to another level. His perfectly fragrant broths perk up blue lobster and shrimp ravioli with a little langoustine bath, or lend new flavor to poached cod. We likewise linger over tiny gratinéed clams with black lemon and seaweed butter, unless we just decide to build our own seafood platter.

36 rue des Petits Champs, Paris 2nd.
Lobster ravioli €29.

MICHO

Why make a sandwich on normal bread when you could make it on Mamiche's challah (that delicious bread served for Shabbat)? That's the highly interesting MO of chef **Julien Sebbag (Créatures, Forest)**, a chef who's as bankable as he is nice. **He's dreamed up an addictive sandwich shop,** where we recommend you arrive before 12:30 p.m. to avoid the line. Paris foodies dive to get the

Crash Kebab with smashed beef meatballs, mixed herb salad, almonds, honey-mustard thina, or the breaded chicken schnitzel with red cabbage coleslaw, black garlic aioli, and arugula.

46 rue de Richelieu, Paris 1st. Sandwiches €13 to €17.

LOULOU

See you at the Tuileries garden, adjacent to the Musée des Arts Décoratifs—this Parisian rendezvous spot features a mind-boggling decor by Joseph Dirand done completely in marble, with Saarinen chairs, 1960s accents, and art deco details, along with an incredible view of Paris and a dreamy terrace right out of a Sorrentino set. You'll rub shoulders with the tony crowd and those young darlings who are thrilled to see and be seen (like the beautiful fashion world people, who've made it their fashion week headquarters). On the menu: **popular Italian cuisine dressed up for evening,** including pipe rigate alla vodka, pizza with truffles, and red prawn carpaccio with Sicilian orange.

107 rue de Rivoli, Paris 1st. Vitello tonnato €26.

Loulou / © Michel Tréhet

Palais-Royal Restaurant / © Guillaume de Laubier

OMAR DHIAB

Be sure to remember the name! Accustomed to big restaurants (Lasserre, Pavillon Ledoyen, etc.), Omar Dhiab, the former chef of Loiseau Rive Gauche, opened his eponymous restaurant next to the Place des Victoires, gaining his first Michelin star immediately afterward. His signature? **Truly contemporary cooking** that honors his Egyptian origins. From appetizers to orange blossom–scented semolina cake (the chef's madeleine), each detail is meticulously thought-out, as is the superb wine list that gives pride of place to small producers. A true find! *23 rue Hérold, Paris 1ˢᵗ. Prix fixe lunch €68.*

PALAIS-ROYAL RESTAURANT

This is a very discreet spot that you might never have heard of before. And yet **Philip Chronopoulos's two-Michelin-starred restaurant deserves to be lingered over** at a sunny lunch in the most beautiful garden in Paris. The kitchen turns out amazing dishes with Mediterranean accents, including a memorable monkfish with saffron, fava beans, and kaffir lime, as well as the huge petit fours (better eat them before they crumble, just like at your grandma's house in the South of France!). We'll gladly acquiesce. *110 galerie de Valois, Paris 1ˢᵗ. Prix fixe lunch €145.*

JARDIN DU PALAIS-ROYAL

Completely removed from all the hustle and bustle, Jardin du Palais-Royal, created under Richelieu and the former residence of the Duke of Orléans, is a ritzy corner of paradise that extends over five acres. Tip: don't get there too late if you want to snag green recliners—they're perfect placed right in the sun next to the fountain. The chic dogs from the neighborhood frolic underneath the trees, a few groups devote their time to playing pétanque in the narrow paths, while others sit on a bench in the fresh air with their heads buried in a book. Meanwhile, fascinated tourists divide their time scaling the black-and-white Colonnes de Buren and taking photos of themselves (we understand why!). Far from the clock and away from the frenzy, this picture-postcard spot is an oasis of calm and beauty we'll never tire of.

2 galerie de Montpensier, Paris 1ˢᵗ. Free admission.

THREE SURE BETS
ON RUE
SAINTE-ANNE

Udon Jubey / © Emanuela Gino

UDON JUBEY

It may not look like much, but this little restaurant makes some of **the best udon noodles in Paris.** You know, those thick, silky white noodles that are dipped into hot or cold broth? Of the vast collection (to do it right, you should try them all), we go for the signature Jubey Udon with soy milk, miso, pork, chrysanthemum, sesame, and Chinese cabbage or the Tempura with shrimp, chives, and lotus flower. Our recommendation? Get there superearly (around 6:45 p.m.) or late (around 9:45 p.m.) to avoid the line. Do what you will with this info: Louis Garrel is a regular.

39 rue Sainte-Anne, Paris 1ˢᵗ. Udon from €13.60.

MICHI

Ask to be seated at the counter, so you can **admire the master sushi chef preparing the fish,** which you'll immediately see is of excellent quality, before happily noting that it all melts delicately in your mouth. In this pint-size omakase, you'll be served sushi and rolls featuring fatty tuna, bonito, sea bass, salmon, sea bream, and scallops . . . like you've never tasted anywhere else. For dessert, try this amazing discovery: an all-pink sakura mochi flavored with cherry flower.

58 bis rue Sainte-Anne, Paris 1ˢᵗ. Deluxe assortment €22.50.

HIGUMA

The hangout spot for Japanese cuisine obsessives. Of course the cafeteria-style decor leaves a bit to be desired. But we take great pleasure in the bowls, which have an unbeatable quality-price ratio. The most fragrant is probably still the shoyu with soy broth. Important: we automatically order a plate of perfectly grilled gyoza, and enjoy the show as they're cooked right in front of us.

32 bis rue Sainte-Anne, Paris 1ˢᵗ. Shoyu Lamen €8.

BONUS:

K-Mart, **the most kawaii supermarket in Paris,** where you can do your shopping as if you were in a manga.

6 rue Sainte-Anne, Paris 1ˢᵗ. Package of chicken gyoza €9.46.

A SPEAKEASY

TO IMPRESS YOUR DATE

Your date won't believe it. Head over to the Hôtel Normandy, known as *Le Chantier* (The Construction Site) since it has remained open during renovations. Behind a hidden door, you need only descend a narrow flight of spiral stairs to discover **Rehab, the hippest and trendiest speakeasy around.** We love to sit on the old opium bed, enjoying the low-lit, sensual decor as we sip incredible cocktails. It's truly a show, with smoke infusions, split glasses, superb garnishes, and novel flavors, including a few potions with CBD.

Rehab, 7 rue de l'Echelle, Paris 1ˢᵗ.
Cocktails €17.

Rehab / © Rehab

3 REMARKABLE ARCHITECTURAL GEMS

The Oval Room at
the BnF Richelieu
5 rue Vivienne, Paris 2ⁿᵈ

The glass rotunda
at Galerie Colbert
1 passage Colbert, Paris 2ⁿᵈ

The sumptuous choir
vault at the Church
of Saint-Roch
296 rue Saint-Honoré, Paris 1ˢᵗ

Bibliothèque de la BNF Richelieu / © Emanuela Cino

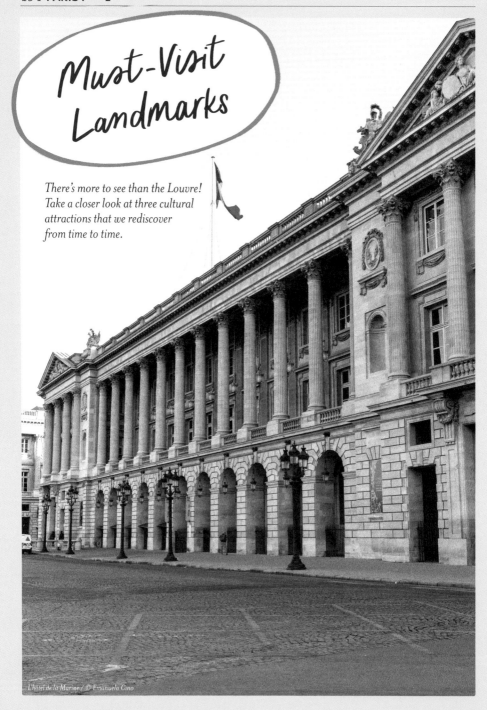

Must-Visit Landmarks

There's more to see than the Louvre!
Take a closer look at three cultural
attractions that we rediscover
from time to time.

L'hôtel de la Marine / © Emanuela Cino

L'HÔTEL DE LA MARINE

The Crown's former storage unit at the Place de la Concorde resembles a Parisian palace. After its time serving as the Ministry of the Navy, this important center of French knowledge and style has been transformed back to its original use. It houses an office, dining room, apartments, and bathrooms that replicate the aristocracy's lifestyle in the eighteenth century. It's a quintessential spot you can visit again and again, especially after you've had breakfast at Café Lapérouse (which is right by the entrance).
2 place de la Concorde, Paris 8th. Full-price admission €17.

LA COMÉDIE-FRANÇAISE

Seeing something by Molière, Marivaux, or Feydeau in the Salle Richelieu of **this legendary theater founded in 1680** should be required by law. Among the thirty shows presented each season, tickets for the repertory's classic comedies go fast, although there are always same-day tickets available to buy at the box office, so you don't need to reserve months in advance. The best French actors never disappoint, from Christian Heck to Guillaume Gallienne, Florence Viala, and Marina Hands (to name only the most famous), who perform in both classic and avant-garde (but never stodgy) productions.
1 place Colette, Paris 1st. Tickets from €6.

MUSÉE DE L'ORANGERIE

You probably know that this elegant museum hidden all the way at the bottom of the Tuileries is home to Claude Monet's majestic *Water Lillies*. But have you ever taken the time to go admire it from the legendary oval room where it takes up every wall? In addition to this poetic splendor, you can discover a permanent collection that includes masterpieces by heavy hitters like **Matisse, Cézanne, Modigliani, Picasso, and Sisley.** You could go for them alone! Think about it the next time you're strolling through the gardens.
Jardin des Tuileries, Paris 1st. Full-price admission €12.50.

La Comédie Française / © Emanuela Cino

Musée de l'Orangerie / © Emanuela Cino

© Geraldine Martens

LATIN QUARTER

It's one of the oldest neighborhoods in
Paris, a student stronghold (since the
Middle Ages!) that extends from the
Place Saint-Michel to rue Mouffetard,
and all the way to Jardin des Plantes.
In addition to its legendary universities
and quays along the Seine (which are
among the most romantic in Paris),
you'll discover incredible places
where food and culture meet.

5th Arrondissement

Clémence Renoux

Osteria Brutto / © Cyril Casagrande

OSTERIA BRUTTO

Inspired by the cult New York spots in Robert de Niro and Al Pacino films, this Italian restaurant breaks the classic trattoria mold with its truly gangster dishes: an extra-crisp Caesar salad, spicy rigatoni alla vodka, veal cutlet parmigiana with tomato sauce and melted scamorza. Purists will also feel right at home, with truffle and Parmesan cream arancini, traditional spaghetti pomodoro with meatballs, or spaghetti with clams, along with beef carpaccio finished with truffled cream and Parmesan. The latest "hit": an affogato with a scoop of fior di latte or hazelnut ice cream.
15 rue Gracieuse, Paris 5th.
Spicy rigatoni alla vodka €14.

OTTO

Inspired by Japanese izakayas, **this new hot spot is the dream child of Michelin-starred chef Éric Trochon** (Solstice) who also **holds the title of** *Meilleur Ouvrier de France.*

He's added a touch of sexy exoticism to the Mouffetard neighborhood. Head over now and start blissing out in the unapologetically minimalist decor (by the architect behind the legendary Sketch in London). You can share clever dishes where fish, meat, and vegetables are used in a play on crispy and tender, various regional cuisines, and the contrast between hot and cold. Plus, a sauce here, an herb there. Note: the wine list has over a thousand options.
5 rue Mouffetard, Paris 5th. Chicken yakitori €13.

BAIETA

Baieta means "kiss" in Nicoise dialect. It's indeed a declaration of love that Julia Sedefdjian offers Parisians, melding her signature cooking with Nicoise eats. Sedefdjian, the youngest chef to be awarded a Michelin star in France (she was only twenty-one!) has made bouillabaieta, an irresistible homemade bouillabaisse, her signature dish. You should try it at least once in your life, along with her aioli, pissaladière, and socca to start. **You can almost hear the cicadas!**
5 rue de Pontoise, Paris 5th.
Signature four-course prix fixe €100.

HÉBÉ AND YA BAYTÉ

It's pretty, fresh, and colorful—in short, you can feel the sun. Welcome to Hébé, the first Mediterranean spot from master of the house Imad Kanaan. Teaming up with his wife, the Lebanese restaurateur commissioned the talents of Marseillais Michelin-starred chef Michel Portos to dream up a menu that is, quite simply, delightful. It includes dishes such as classic roasted red mullet and shoulder of lamb confit accompanied by chickpea salad. Surprise: the spot has been so successful that the couple opened Ya Bayté a stone's throw away, a salute to Imad's soft spot for crazy good street food. In addition to classic falafel and shwarma, it offers delicious stuffed turnovers typical of his native village, Beit Chabab.
Hébé: 15 rue Frédéric Sauton, Paris 5th. Prix fixe €59.
Ya Bayté: 1 rue des Grands Degrés, Paris 5th.
Two fatayer banadoura turnovers €6.50.

HUGO & CO

After the enormous success of Tomy & Co, his signature bistro in Gros Caillou, **Tomy Gousset does it again** in a slightly forgotten corner of the 5th. The result? A meeting place as relaxed as it is stylish, offering a decidedly creative and blended cuisine, designed to be shared: bao with confit of lamb, crunchy tartine with shrimp, miso salmon, and, for dessert, swoon-worthy chocolate ganache and corn ice cream. Fun quirk factor: the wall of wooden crates creates a vibe that's halfway between Parisian chic and New York bar.

48 rue Monge, Paris 5th. Prix fixe with appetizer, entrée, dessert €46.

CAFÉ MAA

A beautifully decorated boutique, gallery, and a totally chill café: the typically Nordic art of relaxing has arrived at the Institut Finlandais! **Its warm and cozy canteen** (with large wooden tables, bouquets of flowers, and works by local artists decorating the walls) offers salmon or marinated herring tartines on rye bread, amazing salads, cinnamon buns, and a Scandinavian pine-flavored chai latte you'll be writing home about!

60 rue des Écoles, Paris 5th. Salad €16.

LA RÔTISSERIE D'ARGENT

Always dreamed of trying the legendary duck at La Tour d'Argent? You're going to adore the rotisserie, **the Michelin-starred restaurant's younger sibling, where they serve exceptional cuisine** from the restaurant that inspired *Ratatouille*—in an accessible version. Not to be missed: the terrace makes you feel like you're floating above the Seine, and its checkered tablecloths and retro feel are still as charming as ever. The menu is a staunch advocate for hearty cuisine canaille, such as duck foie gras with ruby port and pear chutney, escargots de Bourgogne with parsleyed butter and pastis, and duck leg with bay leaves. Wow!

19 quai de la Tournelle, Paris 5th. Half free-range chicken €28.

La Rôtisserie d'Argent / © La Rôtisserie d'Argent

PASSION CHOUX

Delivered in the prettiest, most perfectly shaped rectangular box, **Odette's** cream puffs (an homage to the grandmother of founder Frédéric Berthy) literally melt in your mouth. The cream filling plays on naturally strong flavors—coffee, caramel, chocolate, lemon, mixed berries, passion fruit, pistachio, praline, and vanilla. And the pastry? Yummmmm. Soft but with just enough structural integrity—an incomparable joy.
77 rue Galande, Paris 5ᵗʰ.
Box of six cream puffs from €11.50.

Tram / © Pauline Darley

WE'D CROSS PARIS FOR . . .

TRAM

Surely you noticed this charming café-bookshop in season two of *Emily in Paris* (whose main character happens to live in the Latin Quarter, on Place de l'Estrapade). Everyone loves this absolutely perfect spot, which is both trendy and pretty as a postcard. Just behind the Panthéon, Paul Hyatt and Marion Trama have dreamed up **an inspiring, poetic place with a delightful decor** where you can easily telecommute in the morning, then stick your nose in a book at lunch over a frothy matcha latte, an orange blossom almond milk, or a more-is-more croque monsieur. You'll also find coffee table books on Paris, food, art, and travel, in addition to a grocery area where you can find a bottle of naturally produced wine to take to dinner, along with a Plaq chocolate bar.

47 rue de la Montagne Sainte-Geneviève, Paris 5ᵗʰ. Croque monsieur €17.

FOOD SHOPS

Underneath its intellectual appearance, the Latin Quarter functions like a village in everyday life, with its own set of small, independent merchants.

OUR FAVORITES INCLUDE:

COW

For cheeses from all around the world

30 boulevard Saint-Germain, Paris 5ᵗʰ

LE BONBON AU PALAIS

For luxury confections

19 rue Monge, Paris 5ᵗʰ

BOULANGERIE ARCHIBALD

For the best country bread in the neighborhood

28 rue des Fossés Saint-Bernard, Paris 5ᵗʰ

LES FLACONS

For natural wines that really deliver

34 rue des Écoles, Paris 5ᵗʰ

CARL MARLETTI

For yummy pastries

51 rue Censier, Paris 5ᵗʰ

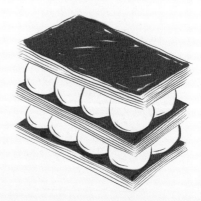

TWO RECORD SHOPS IN TUNE WITH THE TIMES

A piece of advice to those who've invested in a record player ("It's so retro, and the sound is better, don't you think?") but don't really know what to put on it. Head over to **Crocodisc** (*42 rue des Écoles, Paris 5ᵗʰ*), which has gathered the coolest, edgiest vinyls from every genre of music, except classical. For that category, music lovers prefer **La Dame Blanche** (*47 rue de la Montagne Sainte-Geneviève, Paris 5ᵗʰ*), which also specializes in jazz. Paris is going to be swinging!

La Dame Blanche / © Emanuela Cino

Institut du Monde Arabe / © Emanuela Cino

INSTITUT DU MONDE ARABE

It's the most diplomatic cultural center in Paris, whose glass walls were (of course) designed by Jean Nouvel. There are **exhibitions, language classes, a library, studios, and a movie theater.** The incredibly varied programming is always fascinating. Psst: the ninth floor is home to Dar Mima, a festive restaurant with a decor reminiscent of *One Thousand and One Nights*, couscous (such great couscous!), along with live music. Its creative concept was designed hand in hand with Jamel Debbouze!

1 rue des Fossés Saint-Bernard, Paris 5ᵗʰ.

Must-Visit Landmarks

Musée de Cluny / © Emanuela Cino

MUSÉE DE CLUNY

Fans of the courtly Romanticism embodied by Héloïse and Abélard and *The Lady and the Unicorn* will be jumping up and down: Musée de Cluny is beautiful again, having reopened its doors in 2022 with a series of impressive surprises. The museum commonly known as **the Museum of the Middle Ages,** often misunderstood by Parisians, is among the most beautiful historical structures in Paris. The Gallo-Roman baths are two thousand years old, and the private mansion dates back to the fifteenth century. The treasures you can (re)discover include: gold and silver jewelry, including Byzantium-style crowns, jewels from queens, and even secret rooms with vaulted ceilings where women would gather to spread the court gossip.

28 rue Sommerard, Paris 5ᵗʰ. Full-price admission €12.

JARDIN DES PLANTES

A true Eden of plants and flowers, this French-style garden created in 1635 by Louis XIII, planted with remarkable trees, spans no less than fifty-nine acres! Reminiscent of a film set, its elegant Grandes Serres greenhouses are home to a luxurious jungle with everything from robust desert flora to the exotic plants of New Caledonia. After experiencing the dreamy space, go for a stroll in the park through the rose garden, labyrinth, and brightly colored alpine garden. It's sure to brighten up your day on every level.

57 rue Cuvier, Paris 5ᵗʰ.
Free admission, Grandes Serres €7.

LA GRANDE MOSQUÉE DE PARIS

Some people visit this jewel of Hispanic-Moorish architecture, built in 1926, for **its minaret and gardens, with their soft scent of jasmine**—a must-see that will leave you speechless. Others prefer to take a seat in the tree-shaded tea salon, where they can share a few gazelle horns and makrouds. Our secret weapon is to treat ourselves, once a year, to this winning combo: hammam (reserved for women and not for the shy!) + scrub + massage + couscous, beverage, pastry, and mint tea. Spend a day of bliss unwinding with friends at this highly transporting gem.

39 rue Geoffroy-Saint-Hilaire, Paris 5ᵗʰ.
Massage & Saveurs package €90.

Jardin des plantes / © Emanuela Cino

Grande mosquée de Paris / © Emanuela Cino

Ralph's / © Valérie Lhomme

Saint-Germain-des-Prés

Wander along the tree-lined quays, treat yourself to an arty exhibition at a cutting-edge gallery, snatch up a little dress at a pretty boutique or a coffee table book at a cult bookshop, sit down at a subdued Michelin-starred restaurant, or have breakfast on a terrace. Saint-Germain-des-Prés calls for a long, long, stroll!

6th Arrondissement

Clémence Renoux

JAPAN WITHIN REACH

Blueberry / © Gabriel Pistre

BLUEBERRY

With its cinematographic decor inspired by the films of Wong Kar Wai, the stylish Blueberry immediately wows! Run by the Vaconsin sisters (Marcello), this beautiful restaurant is one of the best Asian options in Saint-Germain-des-Prés. For a dozen years now, **its signature sushi rolls have become the hands-down favorite of discerning diners,** who are partial to its salty delicacies, including the iconic Rackham Le Rouge roll featuring marinated tuna, truffle, and prawn tempura. And don't forget the house-made matcha mochi. Fans will be asking for more.
6 rue du Sabot, Paris 6th.
Six-piece Rackham Le Rouge roll €24.

KODAWARI RAMEN

You'll hear some serious slurping at **this eatery, which immediately transports you to the atmosphere of a small street in Tokyo,** complete with a steamy counter where the chef sees to his broths. To avoid the miles-long line, it's better to arrive early—for example, at noon for a weekday lunch! Don't leave without trying the ramen with secret sauce, featuring black sesame, garlic, ginger, and its Iberian chashu pork.
29 rue Mazarine, Paris 6th. Kurugoma ramen €14.50.

BAR DES PRÉS

It may be expensive, but God is it good. An outpost of his bistro on rue du Dragon, TV chef Cyril Lignac dreamed up **this bar inspired by the glamourous hot spots of London and New York.** What do we come here for? Superb cocktails and raw fish in the form of designer sushi and gourmet small plates, all cooked to order from the bar by a superhip brigade while the mixologist busies himself with the potions. Honestly, it's hard to get over the crispy shrimp with wasabi sesame and Thai mayonnaise.
25 rue du Dragon, Paris 6th.
Eight-piece California roll to share €28.

Our Favorite Eateries

Baillotte / © Simon Detraz

ZE KITCHEN GALERIE

Vinaigrettes, broths, and condiments hold no secrets for the **king of creative gastronomy** William Ledeuil. He continues to stun guests at the Michelin-starred restaurant Ze Kitchen Galerie, located near the Pont Neuf, with dishes such as line-caught marinated fish, lobster ravioli, fish of the day in a bouillabaisse broth, guinea fowl with damson plum relish, wasabi white chocolate ice cream. Diners, buckle up for a long and happy ride full of discoveries.

4 rue des Grands Augustins, Paris 6th.
Five-course prix fixe €95.

BAILLOTTE

Rue du Dragon's romantic side is rising again with a restaurant by Japanese chef Satoshi Amitsu, who is offering up **incredibly delicate cuisine that walks the line between bistro and fine dining.** His trick? His poetic, mind-boggling presentations, featuring flavors that are always in balance. With a changing menu (turbot meunière, grilled veal chop, langoustine ravioli, etc.), the regional cooking takes its cues from the Japanese sensibility of the chef and the wines (primarily natural), selected by sommelier Thomas Legrand.

16 rue du Dragon, Paris 6th. Langoustine ravioli €20.

SOURCE

Nestled near rue de Buci, Source has assembled a high-caliber team led by the young chef Jules Recoquillon. He learned the ropes with top chefs and is now delivering truly impressive food. We go all-in for the five-course prix fixe, **which gives carte blanche to the sommelier,** tasked with creating the perfect wine pairings for the changing dishes, including lovely carrot ravioli, celery risotto, and breaded veal. It would not be surprising if a Michelin star is coming soon.

17 rue Grégoire de Tours, Paris 6th.
Five-course prix fixe €75, wine pairing €35.

Brasserie des Prés / © Brasserie des Prés

BRASSERIE DES PRÉS

After having enlivened the Right Bank with its brasseries Bellanger, Dubillot, and Martin, **the Nouvelle Garde group is opening its fourth location** in the structure that was home to the tower of King Philippe Auguste. The group has again found its recipe for success with (as the change to the Left Bank requires) an extra dose of chic in the decor and on the menu, which is chock-full of beautiful, incredibly fresh fish, and even has a dance floor on the third floor. To cool off, visit the adjacent ice cream parlor to satisfy frosty cravings.
6 cour du Commerce Saint-André, Paris 6th. Sausage with mashed potatoes €13.

ROGER LA GRENOUILLE

If you loved La Belle Époque, the great moments of Le Basilic, and used to frequent Le Baron, **there's no doubt you'll love Roger La Grenouille.** Ad execs, producers, members of the social elite, and all the young scions swear by the cheeky menu: a frog burger (tastes like fried chicken!), a ridiculously good tartare with house-made fries, chicken with vin jaune and utterly irresistible morels, all washed down with excellent wine—comme il faut.
28 rue des Grands Augustins, Paris 6th. Frog burger €29.

ALLARD

Founded in 1932 by Marthe Allard, a Burgundy native who arrived in Paris with her family's secret recipes, this legendary bistro is known for having a long line of female chefs in the kitchen: Pauline Berghonnier, Alexia Duchêne, and Laetitia Rouabah. The resident experienced cooks ensure the continuity of a deliciously hearty cuisine canaille (pâté en croûte, Challans duckling with olives, escargots) in an all-red interior that has not changed one bit. **The Beckhams happily return here again and again,** as do all the celebrities who've written their names in the bathrooms!
41 rue Saint-André-des-Arts, Paris 6th. Pie €28.

LE RELAIS DE L'ENTRECÔTE

Paris's smart set is still searching for the secret ingredient in the divine sauce at Le Relais de L'Entrecôte, **the preferred meeting place of all the actors and CEOs of top companies.** No ordering required. The restaurant offers a single, set menu of walnut-topped salad, incredibly tender sirloin with a divine green sauce, and a side of perfectly crispy fries. Everything's paired with organic wines from Château de Saurs, and served in two batches by petite, apron-clad ladies.

20 rue Saint-Benoît, Paris 6ᵗʰ. Prix fixe €26.50.

LIPP

Its bustling, authentic atmosphere is the perfect embodiment of the capital: intellectual, social, and nonchalant. At one time shunned by true Parisians, **this iconic brasserie is now drawing the hottest celebrities,** from Kate Moss to incognito J.Lo and Ben Affleck, not to mention Tom Cruise, Arnold Schwarzenegger, Emmanuel Macron, and Emily Ratajkowski. One room, a thousand ambiances!

151 boulevard Saint-Germain, Paris 6ᵗʰ. Sole meunière €42.

Le Relais de l'entrecôte / © Emanuela Cino

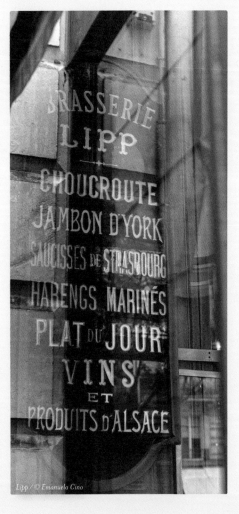

Lipp / © Emanuela Cino

For a Stylish Snack

Café Nuances / © Café Nuances

FOU DE PÂTISSERIE

The concept of founders Muriel Taillandier and Julie Mathieu? **Offer creations from the best pastry chefs in Paris at a single address.** Some standouts that we have enjoyed: Angelina's lemon tart, Bulliz's garnished choux pastry, Pages Blanches's raspberry pistachio tart, Pierre Hermé's iconic Ispahan cake, and Babka Zana's rolls. Yummm. Also delicious—an excellent selection of jams, crunchy granolas, and chocolate bars.

64 rue de Seine, Paris 6ᵗʰ.
Ispahan cake €29.

CAFÉ NUANCES

Although it may be pocket-size, it's the only thing you see in the street, between its mosaic mirror and rainbow ceiling! Located opposite the Théâtre du Vieux-Colombier, **this disco-vibes hot spot pours specialty coffee** in every permutation for the most sophisticated palates. Our favorite? The girly Rose Latte sprinkled with edible rose petals. And to take home, there are five exceptional coffees roasted in Paris and packaged in chic pouches.

22 rue du Vieux Colombier, Paris 6ᵗʰ.
Espresso €2.50.

THREE ICONIC TERRACES

Ralph's / © Valérie Lhomme

LA SOCIÉTÉ

It's the chicest meeting place in the 6th. There's a sublime terrace that always draws a big crowd at the slightest glimpse of the sun and an incredibly elegant interior by Christian Liagre where we have lunch or dinner, happily seated in beautiful armchairs at an impeccably set table. We personally love to keep watch for undercover celebrities, listen to the passionate debates of neighboring tables of gallerists or political personalities, and, above all, take advantage of the flawless service. The Crying Tiger (which is *so* Costes) has already won over Paris's stylish elite.

4 place Saint Germain–des–Prés, Paris 6th.
The Crying Tiger €44. Bottle of Sancerre €70.

LES DEUX MAGOTS

Once upon a time there was Les Deux Magots. Tucked along the cobblestones of the Place Saint-Germain-des-Prés opposite the church, this institution, a haunt of renowned personalities of the last century (Hemingway, Verlaine, Picasso, etc.) is still well loved by the Parisian smart set. Whether you're seated on its majestic terrace or in the large retro-style dining room, **everything tastes a bit classier here.** We love to treat ourselves to an enormous breakfast with a hot drink, breakfast pastries, tartines, fresh-pressed juice, yogurt, scrambled eggs, and fruit salad.

6 place Saint–Germain–des–Prés, Paris 6th.
Petit Jean–Paul Sartre brunch €35.

RALPH'S

The private mansion in the flagship Ralph Lauren store hides the most elegant terrace in Saint-Germain-des-Prés: a sublime cobblestoned courtyard, with fountain, umbrellas, striped banquettes, and rose bushes. The Hamptons-vibe decor contrasts with the interior dining room, which is instead decorated in a hunting-lodge style, with a large fireplace and tartan prints. We order **the great classics of American cuisine:** crab cakes, Caesar salad, or the legendary Ralph's Burger, made from meat raised on Ralph Lauren's own ranch in Colorado.

173 boulevard Saint–Germain, Paris 6th. Ralph's Burger €33.

WINDOW-SHOPPING

ROCK THE KASBAH

Fans of Berber design, welcome to your Valhalla. Located on rue des Saint-Pères, this Saint-Germain-des-Prés boutique banks on the charm of natural materials—colors like beige and ivory, palm trees, weavings, and an abundance of linen. We come to provision for floor-to-ceiling gypset decor, snatching up candlesticks made from olive branches, a giraffe wall hook, lovely sconces made from natural seagrass, a woven mirror, a palm lamp, or a wood and bouclé armchair.

14 rue des Saint-Pères, Paris 7th. Woven mirror €75.

ALLISON

A small, friendly boutique, and a mainstay of the corner of rue de Buci, which sells the gems Allison finds in collections by small brands, like Maison Badigo, or more well-known favorite brands like Jane Wood or Samsøe Samsøe. In addition to the many spunky pieces **(color prints are king here)**, we gladly snatch up pretty accessories to satisfy our appetite for sweet impulse buys. A crocheted bucket hat, leopard pants, a wrap dress, pretty socks, dozens of T-shirts, bags, blouses—there's something for absolutely every wallet!

1 rue de Buci, Paris 6th. Items €10 to €500.

ISABELLE TOLEDANO

This jewelry shop, located near the Pont Neuf, is full of whimsy. Customers are welcomed as if they are friends invited back to the house. In its stone- and wood-filled domain, decorated with large vintage furniture, **the jewels are left and right—everywhere.** It's hard to keep your visit short when you have so many choices! No worries, the proprietress is great at making conversation, and recounts the latest neighborhood gossip while we rummage around snatching up bohemian buckles, large silver pieces, colored pearl necklaces, tiny ear cuffs, and even rhinestone pendants.

40 rue Dauphine, Paris 6th. Large hoop earrings from €56.

Rock the kasbah / © Rock the kasbah

MY FAVORITES

DO IT IN
PARIS

MY FAVORITES

3 SPOTS TO GET EDUCATED

Saint-Germain-des-Prés has historically been considered the most intellectual neighborhood in Paris. It may be literary—but that's not all!

TASCHEN

It's the only boutique in France that has (nearly) all the German publishing house's treasures under one roof, and it has become the store of reference for finding **books focused on painting, fashion, design, and even pop culture.** We spend a lot of time flipping through the books that will soon proudly sit atop our coffee tables, all while keeping watch for the biannual flea-market-style sales, when you can top off your collection at a discount.

2 rue de Buci, Paris 6th. Books from €8.

KAMEL MENNOUR

He's one of the most well-known gallerists in Paris, representing famous artists like **Anish Kapoor, Daniel Buren, Camille Henrot, and Ugo Rondinone.** Inside his two galleries in Saint-Germain-des-Prés, we discover the cream of the contemporary scene, from painting to photography, not to mention the many breathtaking installations. Each visit is a truly wonderful surprise.

47 rue Saint-André des Arts and 5 and 6 rue du Pont de Lodi, Paris 6th. Free admission.

CHRISTINE

In the Mood for Love, Barry Lyndon, Basic Instinct, The Royal Tenenbaums. We come to this legendary movie club **to see arthouse films**—remastered classics from France, Italy, Asia, or North America. We keep an eye on the program online, especially the cycles, festivals, and retrospectives (Kubrick, De Niro, DiCaprio, etc.), which send us straight to another era, miles from those blaring blockbusters.

4 rue Christine, Paris 6th. Full-price admission €9.

TO DANCE ALL NIGHT LONG

ALL NIGHT LONG

PAMELA CLUB

It's _the_ rendezvous place for nighthawks!
The very beautiful club attached
to Alcazar, an almost labyrinthine
construction where you go up and down
stairs all the way to the dance floor. It is
very large, with corners of banquettes
under the stone arches, a dance pole,
and the DJ turntables installed right
in the center. Excellent touch: an
oversize smoking room with disco balls
and delicious cocktails served until
midnight. Tip: arrive right at 10 p.m. to
avoid the line.
62 rue Mazarine, Paris 6th.
Cocktail €15.

10 SPOTS
to name drop

THE SIGNATURE WINE CELLAR AT AUGUSTIN MARCHAND D'VINS

26 rue des Grands Augustins, Paris 6th

THE STUNNING DECOR AT MAISON CARAVANE

27 rue Jacob, Paris 6th

THE SUBLIME FLOWERS AT OZ GARDEN

8 rue de Furstemberg, Paris 6th

THE JAPANESE KNIVES AT KAMA-ASA

12 rue Jacob, Paris 6th

THE SEAFOOD AT HUGUETTE

81 rue de Seine, Paris 6th

THE COMIC BOOKS AT TRAITS D'ESPRITS

35 rue Bonaparte, Paris 6th

CELEBRITY HAIRSTYLIST CHRISTOPHE NICOLAS BIOT

52 rue Saint–André– des–Arts, Paris 6th

THE TAKE-OUT MANAKICHES AT CHEZ LE LIBANAIS

35 rue Saint–André des Arts, Paris 6th

THE ROMANTIC TERRACE AT MARCELLO

8 rue Mabillon, Paris 6th

THE PERFECT SMASH BURGERS AT SPECIMEN

3 rue Guisarde, Paris 6th

GREATER PARIS

The intriguing banlieue are full of surprises
and unique places. Let's go and explore
beyond the city center to get our fill of
culture, relaxation, and excellent eateries.

77, 78, 91, 92, 93, 94

Emmanuelle Dreyfus

2 New Michelin-Starred Places To Remember

VILLA9TROIS

With his one Michelin star, Yaël Demarbre is really giving a shot in the arm to this sleeping beauty of eastern Paris. As soon as the weather gets nice, a greenhouse with citrus, a vegetable garden, beehives, a chicken coup, and a large, shaded terrace provide **promise of an idyllic pause**. In winter, it's with this homey family spirit that we come sit by the fire to enjoy the relaxed signature cooking: spider crab, lacquered sweetbreads, and bone-in pigeon. The young chef knows his range of products and showcases interesting twists on classics with just the right amount of fantasy.

71 rue Hoche, Montreuil (93).
Four-course prix fixe €69.
Six-course prix fixe €89.

OCHRE

In the oldest house on a cobblestoned lane in Rueil-Malmaison, former Top Chef Baptiste Renouard welcomes guests at this white tablecloth spot. Beams, exposed stone, and contemporary artwork (the chef's other passion!) reflect his creative personality and heighten the flavors. Each of his dishes carries with it a story, **a memory accompanied by a bold pairing**. They're visual poems you eat, such as an addictive buckwheat butter that opens a delightful feast, then beautifully concluded with a bold yet airy hot chocolate. Psst: make sure to extend your lovely escape with a stroll through the Parc des Impressionnistes.

56 rue du Gué, Rueil-Malmaison (93).
Prix fixe lunch €55 to €80.
Prix fixe dinner €110 to €160.

JACKY RIBAULT: KING OF THE EAST SIDE

*From Vincennes to Noisy-le-Grand, the **Breton chef built like a rugby player** has opened, in this order: a gourmet restaurant, a brasserie, and a bakery-butcher's shop. A Val-de-Marne resident, he naturally opened L'Ours in 2018, mere steps from the Bois de Vincennes, a true retreat that was quickly rewarded with one Michelin star. His MO? Cooking that is as instinctive as it is meticulous, sometimes infused with Japanese accents. His love for the banks of the Marne led him to open a brasserie in 2021, located in the new, eco-friendly neighborhood of Noisy-Le-Grand, which he coined Les Mérovingiens since the town is home to one of the biggest Merovingian necropolises! Also passionate about vintage items and antiques, Jacky Ribault next imagined a deluxe spot that would be in full swing all day long, with an accessible and hearty cuisine canaille menu. Since he was already happy to be away from the center of Paris, he took the opportunity to open Suzanne et Lucien across the way. At one end of the store you can buy natural sourdough bread made from organic ancient wheat flours, along with breakfast pastries, babkas, or financiers. On the other, choose from hand-selected meats, meatballs, charcuterie, or rotisserie items in a space decorated with vintage furniture and objects. After you've feasted and done your shopping, you can even go down to the banks of the Marne.*

L'OURS
10 rue de l'Église, Vincennes (94).
Prix fixe menus €70 to €150.

LES MÉROVINGIENS
32 avenue Emile-Cossonneau, Noisy-le-Grand (93).
Prix fixe lunch €20.

SUZANNE ET LUCIEN
28 avenue Emile-Cossonneau, Noisy-le-Grand (93).
Sandwiches from €3.

Outdoor Guinguette Cafes 2.0

La guinguette des maquereaux / © Cie Les Maquereaux

LA GUINGUETTE DES MAQUEREAUX

Located on the left bank in Nogent. We bask in the sun **all while enjoying a variety of seafood dishes** (salmon tartare, oysters, shrimp, tarama, etc.) with the appropriate little bit of white wine. Amazing: the option to reserve a boat without a permit or go off for a paddle, or take a stroll along the beautiful strip of homes on promenade Yvette Horner.

Îlot de Beauté — square Tino Rossi, Nogent-sur-Marne (94). Mussels marinières €16.

ROSA BONHEUR À L'OUEST

Feel like taking advantage of one of the very coveted Miss Rosa outposts without the overcrowding that comes with it? Head west to moor up at its cool, arty outdoor café. We especially like to come on Sundays, in summer as much as winter, to enjoy **the gourmet and organic all-you-can-eat brunch**. Whelks, shrimp, oysters, wood-fired pizzas, and tapas make for lively cocktail hours and DJ nights. The boaters have disappeared, but the festive feel is still front and center.

20 quai du docteur Dervaux, Asnières-sur-Seine (92). Pizzas from €9.50, brunch €34.

THE BEST WINE MERCHANT IN FRANCE IS FROM ÎLE-DE-FRANCE!

Head to Villiers-sur-Marne to David Morin, who was declared best wine merchant in France out of four hundred candidates. It's a well-deserved victory for a man who earned his stripes at Hédiard and tastes no less than 7,000 bottles per year. At his boutique, which has approximately 2,800 wines, we whisper our menu in his ear and then he whips out **bottles that make the perfect pairing, and always at a reasonable price.**

44 rue du Général-de-Gaulle, Villiers-sur-Marne (94). Bottles under €20.

Les étangs de Corot / © Michel Figuet

LES ÉTANGS DE COROT

Tucked just behind the Saint-Cloud estate, this Relais & Châteaux property is **a pastoral fairyland.** On the agenda: spa, biking, hiking, or a table at Rémi Chambard's Michelin-starred restaurant for a culinary jaunt through the Île-de-France terroir that's easily accessible via the L line from Saint-Lazare. It's worth the trek, with rooms overlooking the ponds that inspired painter Camille Corot. The ultimate delight? Reserve one of the private lounge suites with outdoor jacuzzi at sunset.

55 rue de Versailles, Ville d'Avray (92).
Rooms from €200.

LE DOMAINE LES BRUYÈRES

Head to the Vallée de Chevreuse to discover the little corner of paradise that Cybèle and Franck Idelot have created. The Californian chef Cybèle, who only cooks with healthy, locavore ingredients, has found the country house of her dreams, where she offers farm-to-table cuisine. The shutters of the five rooms open onto the vegetable garden and fruit trees that are in part used to supply the menu at Ruche, the restaurant located upstairs. The four- or six-course menu is a journey through pure flavors and espouses a zero-waste, direct-supply philosophy, in service of **the signature cooking, which has been awarded a Michelin green star.**

251 avenue de Neuville, Gambais (78).
Rooms from €170 breakfast included.
Prix fixe lunch from €95.
Prix fixe dinner from €135.

LE DOYENNÉ

Approximately twenty-eight miles from Paris, in the heart of the park of the Saint-Vrain chateau, Australian chefs James Henry and Shaun Kelly have deserted Paris to open **a bed-and-breakfast.** Their MO? Cooking with ingredients from their vegetable garden. These newbie farmers welcome guests into what used to be Niki de Saint Phalle's studio, redesigned by the Ciguë architecture and design collective, with its enormous frame, large glass walls, open kitchen, and gigantic wood tables. Feel like extending your stay? Reserve one of the ten rooms to make the most out of your eco-friendly reset.

5 rue Saint-Antoine, Saint-Vrain (91).
Rooms from €225, breakfast included.
Evening prix fixe €95.

LA FOLIE BARBIZON

In 2020 Lionel Bensemoun, former enfant terrible of Paris nightlife, made a 180-degree turn to open **a hybrid location on the outskirts of the Fontainebleau forest** that includes a bed-and-breakfast, a vegetarian restaurant, and an artist residency. Perfect for yoga, meditation, and strolls in the forest, La Folie Barbizon is also the ideal point of departure for discovering the legendary impressionists' village. Note: activities and workshops are offered year-round, tailored to the different seasons and artists in residence.

5 Grande Rue, Barbizon (77).
Rooms from €90.

La maison des marronniers / © Iseult Vertie

YOGA, SOUND HEALING, AND VEGETARIAN FEASTS

AT LA MAISON DES MARRONNIERS

Ris-Orangis might not be the stuff of dreams. And yet there we are, arriving at the RER platform via a walkway that is almost invisible for those not in the know, and propelled onto a dirt path lined with chestnut trees and dotted with old, opulent villas. Alena and Jean-Victor fell for one of the homes beyond the block of houses. The couple had been in the process of changing careers (he to vegetarian cooking, she to yoga and sound healing) and wanted to open a holistic center. "We wanted to share everything we love!" Today, the couple welcome guests to their home, for yoga classes during the week and retreats or festive dinners on the weekends (yoga, sound bath, and vegetarian brunch). **Leave your stress at the door** and allow yourself to be renewed by the break, which is as reinvigorating as it is inspiring. Don't forget to take a dip in the Nordic bath.

10 avenue des Marronniers, Ris-Orangis (91).
Festive dinner €85, retreat €490.

CULTURE IN NATURE

LA CLOSERIE FALBALA AT FONDATION DUBUFFET

The master of outsider art never did anything like everyone else. This anticonformist, who abhorred museums, spent seventy years working on the building to house his Cabinet Logologique. It's an outdoor manifest that can only be visited by appointment, the better to preserve this improbably habitable structure. Intentionally conducive to reflection and meditation, **this secret sanctuary is worth the trip.** Wonder is always on the agenda when you set foot on this black-and-white fortress made of resin and concrete.

Sentier des Vaux, Périgny-sur-Yerre (94). €4.50 to €8, free for children under ten.

LE HANGAR Y

At the edge of the Meudon forest, **the first airship hangar in the world** divides its space between art, nature, heritage, science, and gastronomy. The main building, constructed in 1878 for the Paris Exposition, really wows with its outsize volume and enormous installations. The inaugural exhibit takes a deep dive through the history of flying machines, from Leonardo da Vinci's sketches to contemporary works of art. The visit flows into the park, where some twenty installations (Subodh Gupta, Ugo Rondinone, Kiki Smith, etc.) take center stage around the pond. Lastly, as you dip your toes in the water, you can dine at Perchoir Y, home of Michelin-starred chef Guillaume Sanchez.

9 avenue de Trivaux, Meudon (92). Entry to park €3, exhibition €10 to €19.

LE CYCLOP

It was with the utmost secrecy that Jean Tinguely, Niki de Saint Phalle, and a whole group of artist pals (including Daniel Spoerri) created an enormous sculpture between 1969 and 1994. This **seventy-four-foot steel monster,** which sparkles in the middle of the Milly-la-Forêt woods, looks like Miyazaki's *Moving Castle,* and similarly, makes a ton of clanging noises. The guts of this immense head without a body plunge visitor-explorers into a labyrinthine machine where multiple sound and visual creations made of scrap metal and gears live together. It's a fascinating visit for ages eight and above.

Le Bois des Pauvres, Milly-la-Forêt (91). €8 to €12.

La closerie falbala à la fondation Dubuffet / © Emmanuelle Dreyfus

Le château de Rosa Bonheur / © Château de Rosa Bonheur

LE CHÂTEAU DE ROSA BONHEUR

The most famous of the nineteenth century wildlife painters chose to live at the Château de By, **a stately manor in the heart of the Fontainebleau forest.** This magical place is alive again, thanks to Katherine Brault, the new owner, who has devoted herself to creating a true immersive experience into the private life of the artist, with guided visits, a tea salon, and three guest rooms, one of which Rosa herself occupied. Every summer, there is a festival dedicated to female artists that honors the heritage of this before-her-time feminist.

12 rue Rosa Bonheur, Thomery (77). €10 to €20. €1 for children under six. Rooms from €350 (brunch and visit included).

LE MOULIN JAUNE

Between the railroad tracks and the calm waters of the Grand Morin (the valley that inspired many painters) lies one of the residences of Slava Polunin, more famous for his *Snowshow* and work as a poetic clown than for his idyllic refuge. **Even the fence exudes the scent of childhood.** Silhouettes of cats watching out for guests are merely the preamble to a visit that holds plenty of wonders. Transformed into a design laboratory that celebrates nature, the arts, and fantasy of all kinds, Le Moulin Jaune opens its immense garden-theater from time to time, sending you on a journey to a waking dreamland.

1 sente du Moulin Nicol, Crécy-la-Chapelle, gare Villiers-Montbarbin (77). €25.

DOMAINE DÉPARTEMENTAL DE CHAMARANDE

It's the largest public garden in Essonne, dedicated to art and completely free. Furthermore, it's a five-minute walk from the RER C station! Coined a "remarkable garden," the Chamarande site spans over 242 acres, between the Belvédère forest and the Juine valley, while its Louis XIII chateau is home to an artistic and cultural center. While there are exhibits year-round, summer features events in storytelling, music, dance, film, and boating on the canal, which further enlivens **this green jewel box (which is perfectly suited for picnics).**

38 rue du Commandant Maurice Arnoux, Chamarande (91). Free admission.

Wat Thammapathip © Emmanuelle Dreyfus

WAT THAMMAPATHIP

Thailand, less than an hour from Paris? Improbable . . . but true! Otherwise known as how the Château de Lugny was converted into a pagoda by the Thai International Association of Buddhists in France. Arriving at the site is very impressive, with its paths lined with golden Buddhas and its immense park, where families or groups of friends come to enjoy the best of street food each weekend. While it's inhabited during the year by monks, meditation rooms are open to anyone who wants to sit in quiet reflection.

243 rue des Marronniers, Moissy-Cramayel (77). Thai street food €6.

LA BOUCHE DU ROI

Did you know that at the end of the eighteenth century, Île-de-France was the biggest wine-growing region in France? Julien Bengué and Adrien Pélissié have relaunched wine production in Davron, in the grasslands of Versailles. Today the area produces several wine varieties that can proudly face off against those of Bordeaux and Burgundy. Honest to God! You can visit and taste these nectars directly in the wine cellar, which is open Saturdays, or treat yourself to **a half-day educational wine-making tour** to learn the major principles of organic wine cultivation.

12 rue Saint Jacques Davron (78). Tasting visit €29. Half-day tour €85, lunch included.

OUTSIZE GALLERIES

GALERIES GAGOSIAN

It's a scale that's well known in contemporary art, which gave Takashi Murakami pride of place in 2023. At the foot of the runway at the Paris–Le Bourget airport, Larry Gagosian has **an art gallery, designed by Jean Nouvel** in a minimalist style, that's home to enormous works of art. What's more? A mezzanine allows you to get up high so you can admire the sculptures, installations, and paintings from the various long-term solo shows.

26 avenue de l'Europe, Le Bourget (93).
Free admission.

GALLERIA CONTINUA - LES MOULINS

The most famous of the Italian galleries has installed its blue, white, and red outpost in an old paper mill right in the middle of the countryside. Since 2007, these imposing industrial buildings made of hydraulic wheels, metal beams, and concrete have served as the backdrop for major solo and collective exhibitions. **Daniel Buren, Ai WeiWei, Michelangelo Pistoletto, Subodh Gupta, Antony Gormley, and Anish Kapoor** are regulars.

46 rue de la Ferté-Gaucher, Boissy-le-Châtel (77).
Free admission.

A NEW CULTURAL CENTER IN ROMAINVILLE

A former industrial wilderness transformed into a **temple for contemporary art**— that's the crazy bet the Fondation Fiminco made when it opened an artist residency and exhibition spaces here. There are now no less than seven contemporary art galleries: Air de Paris, Galerie Sator, Galerie Jocelyn Wolff, In Situ– Fabienne Leclerc, 22.48 m2, Galerie D, and Quai 36. The cherry on top? The Frac Île-de-France installed its reserves in this superunique space and opened it to the public. Artist studios and the Coutume Café top off your visit. Located a few steps from the Canal de l'Ourcq, it would be a shame to miss it!

43 rue de la Commune de Paris, Romainville (93).

MY TOP 10

My
Coloring

Illustration: Angéline Melin

Illustration: Angéline Melin

Illustration: Angéline Melin

EVENINGS OUT

ICE CREAM SHOPS

HOTELS

OUT OF THE ORDINARY

PARKS

RESTAURANTS

SHOPPING

FOOD

The publisher owes great thanks to all of the featured locations for providing photographs for this book. In each case, every effort was made to credit those holding photo rights. However, if there were any errors or omissions, the publisher will make any correction brought to its attention in all subsequent editions of this book.

First published in the United States of America in 2025 by
Rizzoli Universe, a Division of Rizzoli International Publications, Inc.
49 West 27th Street
New York, NY 10001
www.rizzoliusa.com

Originally published in French in 2023 as
Do It in Paris: 450 adresses coups de coeur by
Hachette Livre, La Maison Hachette Pratique, Paris
www.hachette-pratique.com

Do It in Paris © Hachette Livre, La Maison Hachette Pratique, 2023

Texts by Clémence Renoux, Céline Durr Dassonville, Sandra Serpero, Delphine
Le Feuvre, Emmanuelle Dreyfus, Clara Caggini, and Pauline de Quatrebarbes,
under the supervision of Véronique Constantinoff

Photographs by Emanuela Cino

For Rizzoli Universe
Publisher: Charles Miers
Editor: Klaus Kirschbaum
Assistant Editor: Emily Ligniti
Managing Editor: Lynn Scrabis
Designer: Daniel Melamud
Translator: Liza Tripp

ISBN: 978-0-7893-4581-3
Library of Congress Control Number: 2024943674

Printed in China
2025 2026 2027 2028 / 10 9 8 7 6 5 4 3 2 1

Visit us online
Instagram.com/RizzoliBooks
Facebook.com/RizzoliNewYork
X: @Rizzoli_Books
Youtube.com/user/RizzoliNY

FSC
www.fsc.org
MIX
Paper | Supporting
responsible forestry
FSC® C104723